God for Sceptics:

Cogent Christianity

By John Benton

Grace
Publications

GRACE PUBLICATIONS TRUST
62 Bride Street
London N7 8AZ
www.gracepublications.co.uk

First published in Great Britain by Grace Publications Trust 2023.

Cover design by Pete Barnsley (CreativeHoot.com)
Cover image: *Doubting Thomas* – Wouter Crabeth II, Public domain, via Wikimedia Commons

ISBN Paperback: 978-1-912154-87-6
         Ebook: 978-1-912154-88-3

Printed and bound in UK by Ashford Colour Press

God for Sceptics:

Cogent Christianity

By John Benton

About the author:

John Benton is married to Ann and is the
Director of Pastoral Support for the Pastors' Academy
at London Seminary.

Contents

Introduction:
Scepticism or cynicism

I heard this story on the radio.

An atheist is driving down a city street, desperately looking for a parking space. The multi-storeys are full. The parked cars are jammed nose to tail along the pavements. Around the roads he goes. There's nothing.

He has an important business meeting. It is with a client about a major deal. His future depends on it and he is already late. To send a text and plead he couldn't park would look really lame. In his extremity he does the only thing he can think of. He suddenly finds himself praying: 'O God, please find me a parking space. I'll go to church, I'll do anything. Please give me a parking space!'

Suddenly, a car pulls out in front of him and there is a space, just perfect. The atheist's response is, 'Don't bother God, I just found one.'

A sceptic is someone who looks at evidence to support whatever is being claimed before he or she accepts it. By contrast a cynic is best described as someone predisposed to reject claims, either before the evidence is heard or in spite of whatever evidence is produced. You could say a sceptic has a discriminating but open mind, whereas a cynic has a prejudiced and closed mind.

We live in the post-Christian society of the Western world and for many people, like the atheist whose prayer was apparently answered when looking for a parking spot, no evidence is going to change what they really think about God. They are locked in to cynicism.

Suspect everyone?

A current popular outlook on life tells us that there is no such thing as the truth.[1] Everything is actually simply a matter of individual viewpoints, personal opinion. We only think of the North Pole as the top of the world because the science of cartography happened to begin in the Northern hemisphere. If it had begun in the Southern hemisphere, we would probably see the world as the other way up. Or again, we have whole university departments protesting that white males may see something one way, but black women will see the same thing totally differently.

The idea is that there is nothing that is true for everybody; individual perception dominates everything. Therefore, according to this stance, we ought to be suspicious when anyone says, 'I want to tell you the truth' or 'Can I share this truth with you?' Such people maintain that there is no truth and that any truth claimant is trying to get you to think like them – in other words to control you, to bring you under their power. With this outlook, the conclusion is that it is actually

---

1   This outlook usually goes under the name of 'relativism' or with a slightly different nuance 'post-modernism'.

better to have a closed mind. It is better to be not just a sceptic, but a cynic. Just shut yourself off and think your own thoughts. If you don't listen to other people, you can't fall for their lies.

Common truth

However, this outlook holds out a rather bleak prospect for the world. Harmony and progress have always proceeded by way of trying to understand the other person's point of view – recognising what it is like to stand in their shoes. But this philosophy would tell us not to bother as it is an impossible task. With no common truth, people are inevitably driven apart.

Also of course, the idea is contrary to the way life is. Two plus two equals four for everyone – whether we would like it to make five or not. The law of gravity applies to everybody – so don't walk off a cliff. Listen to your French teacher and you will learn to communicate with French people. English history only makes sense if you acknowledge that there was a woman named Queen Victoria who reigned from 1837 until 1901. Such things are true for us all.

What I am trying to do here is to push back against the cynical flow. Not everything is merely a matter of opinion. I am encouraging you to accept that there is such a thing as common truth and it is worth pursuing. Evidence – scientific, historical etc. – is to be taken seriously. Don't see conversation with others about truth as a threat. It is worth listening to people – not uncritically, keeping your wits about you – because you can learn what is true. Yes, question people. Not everything people say is true. Use your critical faculties. You don't *have* to believe them. But at least give others a hearing. I am encouraging you to be a sceptic but not a cynic. An open mind is better than a closed one.

Truth about God?

But you might be thinking – 'Yes I can accept that there is universal truth in such areas as mathematics, science, languages or even history, but isn't everything people say about God just their opinions, simply speculation at best?'

The stance of classical Christianity is that it is precisely the common truths we find in fields like science, history and more that lead to a compelling, strongly convincing – that is, cogent – belief in God. That may surprise you. But Christianity has always been a thinking religion which encourages the pursuit of truth wherever it is found. It has cogency.

C. S. Lewis was an Oxford don, an expert in Medieval literature, who wrote the famous *Chronicles of Narnia* subsequently enjoyed by many children. As a young man in the trenches of the First World War he was a firm atheist. He was scared witless by the horrific conflict in which he found himself caught up. But he wrote to a friend, 'I never stooped so low as to pray.' For him, unlike our atheist in need of a parking space, not even the foul trenches, bloody wounds and deafening howitzer shells exploding were going to shake him out of that mindset of cynicism about all things religious.

And yet, at Oxford, befriended by J. R. R. Tolkien, the author of *The Lord of the Rings*, they began to talk together about Christianity. And as they talked, and as Lewis read and thought deeply for himself about their conversations, it wasn't that he was bamboozled into accepting Christianity, but rather that the truth of God's existence and of the reality of Jesus Christ became so obvious to him as to be undeniable.

Reluctant convert

It was not even that he liked the idea of becoming a religious person. He didn't – at least to begin with. It was simply that he realised that God was truly there. The logic was utterly compelling. He wrote, 'In the Trinity term of 1929 I gave in, and admitted that God was God, and knelt and prayed; perhaps, that night, the most dejected and reluctant convert in all England. I did not then see what is now the most shining and obvious thing; the Divine humility which will accept a convert on such terms.'[2]

Later Lewis was to write: 'I believe in Christianity as I believe the sun has risen; not only because I see it, but because by it I see everything else.'[3] In other words, not only does Christianity make sense itself, it makes sense of our world. Christians would say that it is actually the foundation for common truth.

So, I am inviting you to be as sceptical as you like, but, like Lewis, to engage in a conversation about Christianity. What is written in this book is one side of the conversation; your own thoughts as you read are the other. See where it leads you ...

---

2   Taken from C. S. Lewis's biography *Surprised by Joy*, Fount Paperbacks, 1977, page 182

3   Taken from *Is Theology Poetry?* by C. S. Lewis, http://www.samizdat. qc.ca/arts/lit/Theology=Poetry_CSL.pdf accessed 04/09/2023

Chapter 1:
God and the evidence

The thing about reality is that it is self-consistent.

There are no gaps, odd bits or leftovers in any way. There are no inconsistencies as there often are in our dreams and nightmares. And it is this attribute of reality – namely self-consistency – that leads us to the truth. The jigsaw puzzle fits together with no holes or ragged edges. When it all fits together smoothly we know that we have solved the puzzle. We have got to the truth.

The world we inhabit is like that because it functions according to cause and effect. One thing leads to another and the whole thing hangs together. Things that don't hang together are lies.

Convergence

Trained as a scientist my early field of interest was in the area of calculating the energy levels of atomic and molecular electron orbitals. The energy levels of the orbitals can be measured practically from spectroscopy. But what is the theory that explains those experimental results? To find that out the equations must be solved.

Actually the quantum equations are so complicated that they can't be solved by direct methods as, say, with a quadratic equation or simultaneous equations. (Life is often complicated like that.) Instead, you have to begin with a guess. Then you use the quality of reality being self-consistent to help you.

The method goes something like this. You make an educated guess at the variables in the equation. You 'turn the handle' on the equation and get an answer and then compare it with the experimental result. You make another guess and solve the equation again. If this second result is further way from the experimental value than the first one, you make a guess on the other side of your first guess. The result now is hopefully nearer to the experimental answer. So, you make another guess in the same direction and so on. And as you go through this iterative procedure your results come closer and closer together and more importantly closer and closer to the experimental value until finally you have the same answer as the experiment (within the limits of experimental error). When your theory coincides with experiment, you know you have solved the problem. You have the truth. That's how our world works.

And in this illustration, evidence can be seen in terms of the answers generated by the equation. When there is a convergence of your answers you know you are on the right track. The evidence is leading us in the direction of a self-consistent explanation of reality.

The crime scene

We are looking for proof or for facts that lead to a consistent conclusion. The suspect's blood at the scene of a murder where there has been a struggle is an example of evidence. The footprints in the house are an example of evidence that someone came inside. The shoe size fits that of the person under investigation. The evidence fits together.

If someone is convicted of a crime, despite having the wrong blood type and their alibi checking out with the facts, we call that a miscarriage of justice. It would be an impossible oddity. People can't be in two places at once. It would be inconsistent.

The great claim of Christianity is that when we look at all the evidence, we see it is true. The teachings of Jesus Christ and the Bible enable us to properly understand ourselves and the world in which we live. Remember the words of C. S. Lewis: 'I believe in Christianity as I believe the sun has risen; not only because I see it, but because by it I see everything else.' Christianity brings us a self-consistent explanation of things that matches reality. That is what truth looks like.

What is the evidence for that claim? That's what we must think about next.

Making sense of science

The area where most people would want to start when it comes to evidence is probably the area of science. So, we will start there.

The turning point in the birth of modern science took place at around the same time and on the same continent as the rediscovery of Bible truth at the Reformation. Though previously the Greeks, the Chinese and Muslim scholars had made some headway in mathematics and technology, the big step forward in understanding the workings of the world came in Europe between 1500 and 1700 AD, the same period as saw the religious world convulsed by Martin Luther's 95 theses and the rise of Protestantism. This is very suggestive of a link between biblical faith and science. And historians continue to argue back and forth as to its precise nature.

The Feasibility of Science

But whatever the exact connection it is very clear that a biblical worldview gives a solid foundation for science to be a viable and reasonable project. What do I mean?

Scripture tells us of one God over all creation. It means that we can think in terms of a *uni*-verse where the same principles apply throughout the whole. If this was not the case, science would be impossible. You might get one answer to an experiment carried out in London and a different result for the same experiment in Padua or on the moon.

The Bible also tells us that this God is not capricious but a God of order, wisdom, faithfulness and law as well as grace (Psalm 104:5; 1 Corinthians 14:33). This is foundational to the whole feasibility of the scientific project. Because the Creator of the world is faithful and consistent, you will get the same results to an experiment carried out on Friday as you did on Monday.

With such a God as the Bible describes, it makes sense that the same laws apply everywhere all the time. To try to find out what those laws are is therefore a project worth pursuing. We will not be chasing shifting shadows. Because there is one God, there is one constant set of laws.

Further, the biblical view of human beings is that we were originally made in God's image (Genesis 1:26–28) with a mandate to be stewards of his creation. One of the great questions is 'Why should we as human beings expect to be able to understand the world?' Such understanding is not necessary for the evolutionary survival and thriving of other species. Dogs and cats don't understand physics or solve differential equations. Turnips and dolphins don't write blogs on anatomy. They just get on instinctively with life. Why should we be any different? But the biblical truth that mankind is made in the image of God provided the early scientists with reason to think that they could uncover God's laws for the physical world he had made. Because, as the Bible says, we are made in God's image (Genesis 1:27,28), we can expect, in the words of the astronomer Johan Kepler (1571 – 1630) to be able to 'think God's thoughts after him.'

Without God the fact of a rational universe which is understandable to us has no explanation. It is an inconsistent oddity. However, the existence of the God of the Bible makes science feasible. God makes sense of science.

The Science of Life

Science is a fascinating discipline and there are so many areas to explore, from physics and chemistry through to climate change and zoology and more. But, in this book, we only have space to focus on one.

The Bible describes God as not only the Creator (Genesis 1:1) and Sustainer (Colossians 1:17) of the universe but in particular as the giver of life. With him is the fountain of life (Psalm 36:9). Christianity teaches that life on earth is a matter of design.

By contrast, atheists think it emerged simply by accident and fortuitous circumstances. But can life really be explained simply by time and chance? The question must be asked.

Life depends on DNA. This is the huge self-replicating molecule which Francis Crick and James Watson discovered back in 1953. It has a double helix structure – rather like a long, twisted ladder. DNA (deoxyribonucleic acid) contains the instructions needed for an organism to develop, survive and reproduce. All life depends on it. So, the question is, what is the probability of this complicated molecule just happening by accident?

In the 1980s the theoretical physicists Sir Fred Hoyle and his colleague Chandra Wickramasinghe did the calculation and concluded that the probability of such a molecule coming together by pure chance was a staggeringly small 1 in 10 raised to the power 40,000 (multiplied by itself 40,000 times). If the probability of throwing, say a three, with a six-sided dice is 1 in 6, you can see 1 in 10 to the power 40,000 is clearly way off the scale. In other words, it is simply never ever going to happen. At the time the *Daily Mail* reported Hoyle and Wickramasinghe's result under the headline 'There must be a God'.

This finding did not go down well with the atheists wedded to a chance universe. So, subsequently, in 1996, Richard Dawkins published his book *Climbing Mount Improbable*. He agreed with Hoyle, that as a one-off event the fortuitous manufacture of such a molecule is impossible. But, argued Dawkins, the odds are greatly reduced if the molecule came together a piece at a time. To illustrate, think of throwing 20 dice all at once while requiring the result that they all come up as sixes. It would never happen. But suppose, instead, you repeatedly rolled the first dice until it came up as a six, kept that, then rolled the next dice a number of times until that became a six, and kept that and so on. Using this method, it would be possible to get 20 sixes fairly easily. Dawkins argument is that DNA could have come about by chance in a similar way – in stages. With such a method 'Mount Improbable' could be climbed.

However, his idea has never gained traction. There are huge problems. Here are three. First, the different components of DNA are complex themselves. They can't be assumed as 'givens' like the dice in our illustration. It begs the question of how they came about? Second, these building blocks would be difficult to keep. Even if they were favoured somehow by natural selection, like everything else in the universe they would deteriorate with time – it's called the Second Law of Thermodynamics. But if these building blocks don't hang around for a substantial amount of time, then DNA has to come together quickly, and we are pretty much back to throwing all the dice at once. Third, molecules called enzymes are necessary for DNA to be able to reproduce itself. But these molecules are incredibly complex too. Hoyle calculated that even for an enzyme to assemble totally fortuitously we are looking at a probability of something like 1 in 20 to the power 100 – another inconceivably small chance.

So, the reasonable conclusion is that the idea of life by chance is such an incredibly long shot that it really should be discarded. And this is especially true when you realise that not only is DNA so complex, but that the Nobel Prize for Chemistry in 2015 was awarded for the discovery and delineating of how living cells have the ability to repair damaged DNA. Did that come about by chance too? How can systems for error correction evolve in the absence of knowing what is an error and what is not – in other words, without design? It's all too much to believe.

And in what we have looked at so far, we have only scratched the surface of the physical side of life including humanity. We have not mentioned the human brain. Here is another indicator of design. David Nutt is currently Professor of Psychopharmacology at Imperial College London. Speaking on Radio 3 in 2022 he made this telling remark when asked about how much is left to know about the human brain: 'I tell my students I'm not even sure we know the language to ask the right questions about the brain.'[1] It appears when we look at the mental side of human beings, we are met once again with a complexity which is far beyond the rather tired explanation that 'it just happened by chance.'

So, from our brief snapshot, here is evidence that seems to converge most easily around there being an 'Intelligence' behind our existence. Reality points to God. The Bible puts it like this 'God's invisible qualities – his eternal power and divine nature – have been clearly seen, being understood from what has been made' (Romans 1:20).

Contemplating history

Let's move on to consider another area as we think about evidence.

Is history going somewhere? We would love to be able to know or even plan the future. It would be so helpful for

---

1   This was in 'Private Passions' on BBC Radio 3, broadcast 09 Jan 2022, https://www.bbc.co.uk/sounds/play/m001382y accessed 31/08/2023.

mankind. If only we could see what's coming around the corner? But when we ask such questions, we have to face the fact that actually we are not very good at predicting the future or knowing where things will lead. History humbles us.

Marxism

Karl Marx (1818 – 1883) thought he had seen the future. The stimulus for human action, he thought, is fundamentally economic. People have to eat and have shelter. In nineteenth century Europe, the ruling class, or bourgeoisie were in charge and the working man often barely had enough to live on. 'This must change,' Marx rightly thought. He imagined it was inevitable. Marx saw his mission in life as being to ignite a class struggle, a revolution of the have-nots against the haves, in order to bring about an equal and fair society. That was the theory.

But the reality of Communism has been very different. The reality is that wherever there has been such a revolution the result has been dictatorship, often tyrannical and crushing in its outworking. There has not been the establishment of justice. His predictions failed. In fact, millions and millions of people have been exterminated under Communism.

And the struggle still goes on as cultural Marxists and politically correct activists push the sexual revolution in our day with the aim of destabilizing normal family life and therefore the Capitalist West. However, the outcome so far hardly seems to be equality, but rather oppression. Many ordinary people live in fear of saying the wrong thing and, for example, being bullied on social media or even losing their jobs.

When we think we can see or plan where history is going, it frequently seems to take a U turn.

Technology

Let's take another example. My father-in-law was an industrial chemist during the middle years of the twentieth century. He was a key man in the early development of materials like nylon. For that reason, he was never able to fight with the forces during WWII. He tried, on a number of occasions to join up, but as soon as it was realised what he did, he was told he was too valuable as a scientist to the war effort. His expertise was crucial in the mass production and improvement of things like parachutes. The whole plastics/polymer industry has moved on vastly since his day. Plastics, rightly used, are extremely versatile and helpful materials. But no-one foresaw what would happen if the world became too dependent on them. We now have a terrible global problem around plastic pollution. We could not see where the future would lead.

A similar story could be told, of course, around the invention of the internal combustion engine and climate change driven by the carbon dioxide from car exhausts.

Technology is something human beings do wonderfully well. We see it as the key to progress. Yet it too has a track record of failing to take us to the destination we hoped for. So apart from the rather ambiguous prospect of where artificial intelligence and all the rest may lead us – we ask again, 'Is history going somewhere?' It is impossible for us to predict.

The Bible

And yet by contrast the Bible shows unparalleled achievement in predictions that come true.

Christianity is founded on the Bible. It is Christianity's textbook. And this remarkable book has two components. These are called the Old Testament and the New Testament. Though it begins with the creation of all things, the main body of the Old Testament is a history of the Jewish nation from about 1800 BC up to approximately 400 BC. The New Testament tells of the life of Jesus Christ, who began his public ministry in AD 30, and then records the spread of the early church.

The Bible tells us that soon after the creation of the world things went drastically wrong as mankind rebelled against God. But the reason the Old Testament focuses on the Jews is that God chose them to be the vehicle through which the human race would be rescued. To Abraham, the founding father of the Jews, God made a promise that from his people the Messiah, the Rescuer would come. So, all the way through the Old Testament we find predictions of the coming of 'the Messiah', what he would be like, what he would do and the consequences for the world. The New Testament's message is that Jesus of Nazareth is the Messiah prophesied in the Old Testament.

At this point, the central feature to keep your eyes on is that gap (of approximately 450 years) between the end of the Old Testament and the beginning of the New. The Bible was not written by one person or by a group of people who could collaborate with each other to make sure their stories matched. Apart from many other factors, the 450-year gap makes that impossible. If the Bible is true, what we are confronted with here is actual prediction which is fulfilled.

Furthermore, in the mid-twentieth century clear evidence for the reality of the 450-year gap was literally brought to light. In November 1947 the Dead Sea Scrolls were discovered in desert caves in Palestine. Over the years some 100,000 fragments and 900 manuscripts have been found. Many of these writings are over 2000 years old, some from the second and third centuries before Christ. Scholars believe they were buried in the caves by a Jewish sect when, after the Romans destroyed Jerusalem in AD 70, the Tenth Legion moved south into the Judean desert in search of the last stronghold of the Jewish rebels. The religious sect wanted their documents to be preserved so they hid them.

Astonishingly, among those documents rediscovered twenty centuries later, are multiple copies of more or less all the books of the Old Testament. These were written over a period of time, somewhere between the third century BC and the first century AD when the Roman army came. One example is what is known as 'The Great Isaiah Scroll', dated, using both style of handwriting and radiocarbon dating, as somewhere between 350 BC and 100 BC. So, we know for certain that this was written way before Jesus was born.

The fact we must grapple with is that what the Old Testament declares concerning the Messiah, comes true, according to the New Testament in the life, death and resurrection of Jesus. Where the Old Testament prophet Micah said the Messiah would be born, Bethlehem, he was born. The prophet Daniel foretold when the kingdom of God would begin, and that is when Jesus came, according to the New Testament Gospels – during the Roman empire, the fourth empire from Daniel's day. King David, a forerunner of the Messiah, predicted in the

Psalms that he would die as his hands and feet were pierced, and Jesus died by crucifixion. The prophet Isaiah said he would be buried in a rich man's tomb, and it happened. Again, Isaiah predicted that after the suffering of his soul he would see the light of life, and the tomb of Jesus was empty three days after he was buried, and his disciples testified that they had seen and met Jesus risen from the dead.

Now, of course, cynics would argue that what the New Testament records need not be true, but were specifically written to make it look like the Old Testament prophecies had been fulfilled. However, many of those early disciples of Jesus who wrote the New Testament were persecuted and died for what they declared about Jesus. They could not have given greater proof of their honesty and sincerity in what they preached and wrote.

But here is the clincher. We don't have to go back 2000 years to see whether or not the Bible's predictions come true. Three simple facts which point to the Bible foretelling the future are right in front of our eyes now.

- First, the Bible tells us that the Jewish race will be preserved until the end of time. Many ancient peoples are lost to history. But the Jews are not – despite the many pogroms and persecutions, not to mention the abominable Holocaust of the mid-twentieth century. These special people are still with us, just as the Bible predicts.

- Second, the Bible tells us that following the coming of the Messiah, people from all nations would turn to God. Christ's church would be a worldwide church. We have been privileged to see that come true as never before

23

over the last two centuries. Who would have thought that in Communist China an underground church of millions upon millions of people would have grown in the last 60 years? And it is a similar story in India and the continent of South America. Two thousand years ago, the Bible foretold this (e.g., see Revelation 7:9).

- *Third*, Jesus made it plain that his church would be persecuted. Alongside the growth of the church there would be martyrdom and rejection. Though the church has often been the prime vehicle through which such things as hospitals, education and women's and children's rights have been brought to the world, nevertheless, despite these good things, the church is often the suffering church. In recent years we have seen Christians targeted by both Communism and extreme Islam. And even in the West, now dominated by 'Woke' attitudes and political correctness, churches who are faithful to the Bible are under great pressure to give up their beliefs or be vilified. But this is all as Jesus said it would be (e.g., see Mark 13:9–10).

The Bible's predictions are realised. Its promises are fulfilled. It seems the future can be known. And that looks very much like evidence that there is a living God.

What to make of Christian experience?

So, the evidence begins to make a case for God. But added to what we have briefly seen, there is something more. Life isn't all about logic and reasoning. There is experience.

You can get to know Christian people with stories to tell about what God had done in their lives.

She wondered what was happening

One of the most remarkable for me concerned a friend named Bunty. She was a middle-aged married woman when I first got to know her with three adopted children. Years before she had been dying. She was in a wheelchair with an aggressive cancer and the doctors had done their best but said there was really nothing more they could do.

But one morning alone in her house, facing the end, she prayed and surrendered her life to Jesus hoping that when her time came, he would take her to heaven. That's unremarkable. But then something happened. Quite unexpectedly, after praying, she began to be aware of what felt like warm water being poured over her. She wondered what was happening. Astonishingly, within minutes she felt strong and got up out the wheelchair – she had been healed. When her husband, John, came home and understood what had happened his first reaction was to say, 'Oh no! Does this mean we'll have to go to church?' Well, it did. And later he became an elder in our congregation in Guildford. Bunty lived for many more years as an active Christian, opening up her home especially for hospitality.

This woman's experience is unusual. But it speaks of the reality of God – a God who is there, a God who hears our prayers.

Here's a lesser but still remarkable experience which I witnessed first-hand.

Friends in Kenya

Beginning in the early 1990s, my wife and I and a small group from our congregation started to visit Christian friends in a poorer part of Kenya near the city of Kisumu. We would teach what the Bible has to say on various topics including family life and marriage. We had the privilege of being instrumental in the building of proper school accommodation for the local children near the village of Kajulu not far from the shores of Lake Victoria.

Things have changed very much in Africa in the last 40 years. But in the days I am speaking about, it was still not always easy to get around. It was straightforward to fly to Nairobi, the capital, but how were a group of eight or nine of us to get up to Kisumu with all our baggage. The train was rickety and slow. Maybe, missionary friends could have taken time to drive us over the unmade dirt tracks into that part of the country, but it would have taken a lot of their time and at least two or three vehicles. It didn't seem fair to ask them. So, what should we do?

With the trip still some months away, we started praying that God would sort the problem out for us. The first thing that happened seemed to be the very reverse of what we were hoping for. One of our group, Pablo, a doctor who worked for a pharmaceutical company, lost his job. We did not know what to make of this, but we prayed on, including his need to find a new position on our list of requests.

After some time, new work opened up for him and this is where a remarkable thing happened. On the first day of his new employment, he was introduced to a woman who would work as his secretary. This lady was from Kenya. That made him think. Inevitably, fairly soon, he talked to her about our proposed trip to her home country. The problem of transport from Nairobi to Kisumu for our group came up. Her response took him aback – and the rest of us when we heard about it. 'That's no problem!' she said. 'My brother, an ex-Kenyan Airforce pilot, now runs a little internal airline in Kenya – he's a Christian and will be happy to get you up to Kisumu at no expense.'

And it all worked out just as she promised. The trip was a success and we felt that God's hand had been at work in it all. Our prayers were answered.

You may, like the cynic we mentioned at the beginning of the book, be unimpressed by answered prayer and try to explain such experiences away. But, if you are a sceptic, though all this might seem very left field for you, I want to suggest that you should not dismiss this but take God seriously.

Science, history and experience make a cogent case for God.

Chapter 2:
Evil?

Every politician and every voter knows that the world is not as it ought to be. This is the starting place for all election campaigns. Political parties promise to improve things.

There is injustice and deprivation, and we can make things better. There are hospitals and schools that could be upgraded. There are people who are unfairly discriminated against and need recognition and help. There are powerful people who misuse their capabilities and need to be held to account. The list is long. But when we look at what is wrong with the world, it seems to go a lot deeper than things which can be fixed by simply voting in a new government. We have been voting against injustice and sin for centuries, but we have made very little headway. How does the evidence of evil fit with Christianity?

Not a materialistic category

Some time ago I was asked to attend a few meetings of a 'think tank' run by an organization called *Civitas*. This group was set up to study civil society. We met near Waterloo station in London, and it was an interesting experience to listen in and try to contribute as some very intelligent people spoke about and discussed the various problems of the day.

During one of those meetings I found myself sitting next to a man who was a professor at the London School of Economics. We got talking during a break in proceedings and introduced ourselves and so he became aware that I was a Christian involved in leading a church. He was from a Jewish background although not religious. Almost inevitably the Holocaust came into our conversation as many of his family had died in the Nazis' concentration camps. But his comment about these atrocious events was striking. He said it was the industrial murder of 6 million of his own people that had forced him to take seriously the possibility of a spiritual/unseen dimension to our world. He explained that though he was not religious, yet he could not reconcile himself to simple materialism as a philosophy of life. I cannot recall his exact words, but he said something like this: 'I know evil is real and I also know it is not a materialistic category.' From the horror of what was done in places like Auschwitz he realised there is something about evil which does not make sense in ordinary terms. There was something from 'outside', perhaps 'supernatural', about this vast wickedness that terminated so many innocent people's lives.

My professor friend found the depth of evil inexplicable and left him unsure about his philosophy of life. Behind the eyes of the killers or the torturers there appears to be something else. The perpetrators of the Holocaust, at least for the moments of their crimes, became somehow 'inhuman'. But the terrible truth is that they were human.

A very similar thought was expressed by the Nobel Prize winning author of *Lord of the Flies* William Golding, in a lecture he gave in Los Angeles in 1961. This is what he said:

> Before the Second World War, I believed in the perfectibility of social man ... but after the war I did not because I was unable to. I had discovered what one man could do to another. I am not talking of one man killing another with a gun, or dropping a bomb on him ... I am thinking of the vileness beyond all words that went on, year after year, in the totalitarian states. It is bad enough to say that so many Jews were exterminated in this way or that, so many people liquidated – lovely, elegant word – but there were things done during that period from which I still have to avert my mind lest I should be physically sick. They were done not by the head-hunters of New Guinea or some primitive tribe in the Amazon. They were done, skilfully, coldly, by educated men, doctors, lawyers, by men with a tradition of civilization behind them, to beings of their own kind ... I must say that anyone who moved through those years without understanding that man produces evil as a bee produces honey, must have been blind or wrong in the head.[1]

Golding's words ought again, to make us think. The level of brutality and sometimes the enjoyment of inflicting pain on others is way beyond the violence which might be required to simply dispatch our enemies. It is so much more than what might be argued in evolutionary terms to be rid of those seen as challenging our survival. The theory of evolution only requires for others to be removed, to die, not that they should be exposed to extreme, prolonged pain and degradation. Once they are out of the way we can survive and thrive. But that is

---

1   *The Great British Dream Factory*, by Dominic Sandbrook, Penguin, 2015, page 344.

not what is going on here. Something other than a mere fight for existence is frequently at play when it comes to human evil.

Jane Austen and Dorothy Parker

However, you do not have to look to the outer limits of evil, like the Holocaust (or the killing fields of Cambodia or, more recently, the mass graves in Ukraine after the Russian invasion) to see the irrationality and malevolent otherness of evil. There are lesser degrees of wickedness where this can be seen too. Evil is much closer and more mundane than we like to admit.

For example, we all know that you do not have to attack another person physically in order to harm them. Mere words can be enormously damaging. 'You are a stupid idiot!' 'You are a walking disaster and always mess things up!' 'You are a slut, and you will never be any different!' Such expressions being shouted at us or just said to us by people of significance in our lives can stick with us permanently. This can cause deep damage. The results are frequently that we become people who have a constant down on ourselves or lack confidence. Psychologists would tell us that our self-image has been perhaps permanently injured. If the recipients of such descriptions of themselves are to get past the impact of such things, it takes a lot of hard work mentally and psychologically. Almost unconsciously a person can think, 'I am that stupid idiot, because that is what my Father/Mother/Friend/Teacher said I am.'

Yet knowing the damage our words can inflict on others, none of us are capable of fully controlling our language, or taming our tongues (see James 3:8). We hurt others almost every day. From deep within us out come our derogatory comments. Indeed, we even applaud the devastatingly acerbic and mocking put-downs of TV comedians and the like. Evidently, we think it is fun to demean people.

When the American writer, Dorothy Parker, was told that President Calvin Coolidge had died, her response was 'How do they know?' The implication was that he was so uninteresting and deadly boring even while he was alive. We find such comments funny.

In her great novel *Emma*, Jane Austen has the title character Emma Woodhouse making a complete fool of the impoverished middle-aged spinster Miss Bates during a social outing to Box Hill. To pass the time in the company an entertainment is proposed that each person should say one thing very clever or two things moderately clever or three things very dull indeed. The lowly Miss Bates remarks, 'Oh, very well, then I need not be uneasy. "Three things very dull indeed." That will just do for me you know.'

But reflecting what human nature is like, Austen, the consummate novelist, tells us that Emma could not resist replying: 'Ah! Ma'am but there is a difficulty. Pardon me – but you will be limited as to number – only three at once.' When the import of Emma's remark dawns on her, Miss Bates is embarrassed beyond measure – blushing with humiliation. Later, of course, Emma is mortified by her vicious jest – especially when the gallant Mr. Knightly confronts her with 'Badly done Emma.' But, of course, she already knew it was a bad thing to do, but nevertheless she could not stop herself.

The fact that we can laugh when other people are made fools of, and yet we would hate to be made fools of ourselves, has an illogical wickedness about it. But even when we recognise that, we still are not always able to control ourselves. And this has nothing to do with intelligence. Often the cleverest people can be the most vicious verbally. Something is going on, even at this very ordinary level, which is hurtful and evil and seems to have a life of its own.

The power of the Ring

The Lord of the Rings is said to be the most popular novel of the twentieth century. The idea that evil has a powerful and corrupting life of its own, is portrayed in a masterly way by J R R Tolkien in his intriguing epic fantasy.

If you know the story, a great ring of evil power has been forged by the Dark Lord, Sauron. However, it falls into the hands of a creature named Gollum. His original name was Smeagol, but possessing the ring for a long time, the change in his name to the guttural 'Gollum' denotes the skulking, slippery, murderous, predator he has become under the ring's power to corrupt. Through Bilbo Baggins the ring leaves Gollum and is inherited by Bilbo's nephew Frodo who is charged by the wizard Gandalf and the wise elves with destroying the ring in the fires of Mount Doom under the very nose of the Dark Lord.

Accompanied by his faithful servant Sam, Frodo bravely and sincerely sets out on the quest carrying the ring. But from both need for guidance and pity, Frodo allows Gollum to join them in the latter stages of their journey. Gollum is addicted to the ring – his 'precious' – and is hoping to slyly get it back.

The historian and social commentator Dominic Sandbrook unfolds what begins to happen towards the book's climax: 'But while there are hints that, were it not for his addiction, Gollum might be more like Frodo, Tolkien shows how, under the influence of the Ring, Frodo is becoming more like Gollum.

Being a decent, humble sort, Frodo has a better chance than anybody else of holding out against the power of evil. But ... *The Lord of the Rings* shows very clearly that not even the most righteous are safe from the demons that lurk within us all. Increasingly irritable and erratic, Frodo becomes fixated on the Ring, even calling it his 'precious', as Gollum does. And in the novel's climactic scene, when Frodo reaches Mount Doom and prepares to destroy the Dark Lord's magic weapon, his resistance crumbles completely.'[2] He decides to keep it.

Thankfully that is not the end of the story. But part of the fascination of *The Lord of the Rings* concerns this corrupting dynamic of evil which we have all experienced. We all, like Frodo, know what it is to be tempted to do things we know we should not do. There is part of us which responds positively to wickedness. And we know what it is to give in and go against our conscience as we feel the power and attraction of evil is too much for us. Even though in a fantasy setting, Tolkien's book becomes a mirror in which we see ourselves. It exposes the power of evil and what we as human beings are like. The book understands us. That is partly why it is so popular. Although it is a fantasy it is real.

A dilemma

If we now see something of the sense of what my LSE professor friend meant when he said that he could not see evil as a materialistic category – that though we participate in it, there is something from outside about it – then for many people,

---

2 *The Great British Dream Factory*, by Dominic Sandbrook, Penguin, 2015, pages 347–348

that leads them to blame God for the origin of evil. If something is beyond the natural, then it must come from God they think. They see evil (both physical and moral) as an undeserved, nasty part of his creation. This would include both suffering and sin. They use this to excuse themselves and to blame the Almighty.

A few years ago, the actor, celebrity and writer, Stephen Fry, famously used this kind of argument in a tirade against God in a TV interview. 'Bone cancer in children. What's all that about? How dare you create a world of such misery! God is a maniac,' he said.[3]

And I'd have to say I would agree with Stephen Fry if God had made the world as it is now. But that is not what Christianity teaches. That is definitely not what the Bible says. Fry was attacking a straw man. Evil exists but the Bible is very clear that it does not come from God. Nor did God make the world in its present state. Fry did not make the case against the God of the Bible that he might think he has. He only made a line of reasoning against a God of his own imagination.

The same argument, that moral evil must be God's fault too, is sometimes used by people to justify their sins. They say something like 'Well I know it's wrong, but I can't help it. It's just the way I am.' They may even go so far as to say, 'It's simply the way God made me.' So, the argument is pushed that it would be wrong for anyone to condemn what they are doing.

However, this is a very dangerous line to take. Such logic can be used not only by, say, the lothario to justify his womanizing but (though most people would rightly throw their hands up in horror) it could be used just as easily by the paedophile to show

---

3 *The Guardian*, https://www.theguardian.com/culture/2015/feb/01/stephen-fry-god-evil-maniac-irish-tv accessed 31/08/2023.

that his own actions are not to be condemned by others. 'I can't help it. It's just the way I'm programmed.'

We would seem to have hit a dilemma. If we use the argument that blames God for evil then not only are we ignoring what the Bible says concerning God, but we have no basis on which to hold people responsible for any of their actions – hence no basis for civil law. What then would happen to our society? On the other hand, if we don't blame God for evil – then that would seem to mean that we are responsible for it – and so can control it and get rid of it. So why haven't we done that when it is such a blight on humanity?

Indeed, advances in medical science have made a big difference in providing answers for physical evils such as diseases. And we need to note at this point that Jesus would have been right on side with that. He did not see pain and illness as part of God's original good design – as per Stephen Fry's argument. Rather he fought those things. Many of his miracles were such as to heal the sick – the blind, the lame and the lepers.

But whereas medical science alleviates physical evil, there is little or no evidence the world is getting better morally. Humanity still manages to produce vast evils. There are still wars. There is still greed. There is still arrogant pride. The better side of human nature is often eclipsed by the dark side. Even though we live in the twenty-first century we can hardly claim to have mastered evil in any way. For example, along with much good, the worldwide web and digital technology have brought with them such things as cyber-bullying, online pornography, nihilistic websites which encourage suicide and internet fraud etc. Human nature hasn't changed. We have simply found new ways of pursuing the same old sins.

We must face the fact that there is something uncomfortably perplexing about human beings. This was signalled by a series of experiments carried out by the Yale University psychologist Stanley Milgram back in the 1960s. People from all walks of life were induced to take part in an experiment which purported to be about the relationship between learning and punishment. They were told by a doctor in a white coat (symbol of medical authority) to try to 'teach' a learner situated in an adjoining room whom they couldn't see but could hear. If the learner got things wrong the 'teachers' were to administer an electric shock. The learners were in fact actors and though no electric shock was actually suffered, they responded with screams and howls when it was indicated that a shock was being applied.

Of course, the real experiment was on the teachers. They could increase the power of the shock for repeated failures by the learners. The experiment showed quite clearly that most ordinary people were prepared to inflict what they perceived as incredibly extreme pain on others rather than defy the authority figure in the white coat. In other words, they cared more about themselves possibly getting told off by the doctor than the pain they inflicted on others. The experiment appalled academics not only because of the questionable methods used but more because of its gruesome results and what it said about humanity. We are not the people we would like to think we are. We are no strangers to evil.

Where does evil come from?

So where does this get us? It appears we are landing in a position of saying that evil, which plays an immense part in our world, has something of a life of its own which is not from God and yet with which we willingly cooperate.

It looks like it is less powerful than God – and yet more powerful than human beings. We are vulnerable to it, seduced by it, complicit with it.

We have to say that it is less powerful than God, because if it were more powerful it would be the equivalent of God itself. But if evil was God, we would expect our world to be a far worse place than it is. There are unspeakably terrible things in our world, but there is also real beauty and joy. There are still gorgeous sunsets and moments of wonderful human kindness. There is calamity and wickedness, but it is contained. It is huge at times, but it never seems to totally dominate. Always, good still is there to be found. Evil is powerful, yet it appears not as powerful as God. But having said that, we also have to acknowledge that evil is not something we humans can ultimately control. It is more powerful than us. So where does it originate?

There are three things to say here:

First, interestingly the Bible never gives us a definitive answer. Evil entered our world as the first human beings were deceived by it. But the implication of the Genesis account is that it already existed. Our world changed when mankind rejected God and welcomed evil. That was when the happy and wholesome creation that God made was corrupted. That is when human nature changed for the worse. That is when the door was opened to disease and natural disasters. Theologians call this event 'The Fall'.

Second, it makes sense to understand that there is a personality behind evil. As we have said, evil has a life of its own, but it is often able to outwit us or seduce us. These abilities are not those of a mere impersonal force. Impersonal entities, mankind is able to investigate, understand and in the end often master. But evil is not like that. This points in the direction of there being a mind behind it. We face a supernatural intelligent darkness. Just as there is a person – God – behind the creation of the world, so there seems to be a person who instigates evil. Of course, of this person the Bible uses the words 'Satan' or 'the Devil'. He is less than God, but the Bible indicates that somehow this person who drew humanity to reject God at the Fall had done the same thing himself.

Third, that we and our world have, at a deep level, fallen under the influence of evil is the fundamental assumption from which Christ and Christianity take their cue. Christ has come to 'save' us – to deliver us from evil as the Lord's Prayer says. And this is a most urgent matter. There are eternal consequences if we are not rescued. As we have noted already, evil seems to have a life of its own and as it has persisted throughout world history, it seems to be a life which does not die. It is a quirk of our English language, but the word 'evil' is what we get if we spell 'live' backwards. To live as God made us is to grow, develop and flourish. To be caught in the life that is backwards, the life of evil, is to be caught up in a continual unravelling, a continual cycle of one step forward and two steps backwards. We experience decay and painful despair. This is hell. Being imprisoned in that forever, is what we all need rescuing from.

It is this understanding of evil which is the base line and starting point for Christ and Christianity.

Chapter 3:
The Father we long for

Is God just a figment of our imaginations? We have thought about all the evil and tragedy in the world. Is a Divine Being just a comforting idea we have dreamed up in order to help us and to give us hope that though life is chaotic and painful it will all be alright in the end?

Hopefully we have already provided enough factual evidence in our first chapter for the existence of God to show that this is not the case. However, it is worthwhile to think about the merits of this challenge to faith and to consider it on its own terms. Is God simply an imaginary comfort blanket? Is he just a fanciful placebo for broken or near-broken hearts?

Some unknown joy

The human condition does include a certain sadness linked to a yearning for something beyond ourselves, something ultimate, outside the ordinary and temporary. The German language has a special word for this. It is the word *sehnsucht* and speaks of a longing for some unknown joy or an aching desire for wholeness which we don't seem to be able to find.

This experience has been known since ancient times. To explain it the philosopher Plato proposed a myth that once there were such creatures as spherical human beings. In his *Symposium* he describes a fictional banquet at which the famous comedy poet Aristophanes gives a speech about Eros the god of love. He describes human beings as being originally spherical with four hands, four feet and two faces on one head. However, in their pride these primal people wanted to climb to heaven. For this, the supreme god, Zeus punished them by dividing each of them in half. These halves are the men and women of today. Thus, we suffer from an endemic sense of incompleteness.

Plato, through the fictional words of Aristophanes, explains that our longing for our former wholeness is shown in erotic desire which aims at union.

It is an intriguing story. But of course, the experience of the human soul is such that even sex cannot ultimately satisfy our deepest needs. Indeed, to place the burden for your own total fulfilment on another human being is to ask too much of them. That is how many relationships go wrong. After all, our partner is only human – like us.

The Shawshank Redemption

This instinctive longing of the human soul for something more also has its contemporary manifestations and illustrations too. For example, if you have ever seen the 1994 movie *The Shawshank Redemption* – a film with the theme of hope – there is a very poignant expression of *sehnsucht* in the story.

The film is about Andy Dufresne, an ex-banker, wrongly convicted of the murder of his wife and her lover. He is given two life sentences in the grim and brutal confines of Shawshank Prison. But there is a scene in which, having won some privileges with the prison staff through his help with their tax returns, alone in the office, Andy takes a disc, puts it on the Warden's record player and switches on the microphone for the loudspeaker system across the prison. The music is a rich and vibrant piece of opera.

It is a duet in Italian, *Duettino Sull Aria*, sung by two women.[1] Their gorgeous voices suddenly resound around the corridors, into the cells and the yard of the prison. It is an electrifying moment. The dull sadness of prison life is interrupted. Everyone instinctively stops what they are doing, stands still and listens, awestruck. Andy's friend, Red, describes the scene, 'I have no idea to this day what those two Italian ladies were singing about. Truth is, I don't wanna know. I would like to think they were singing about something that was so beautiful it can't be expressed in words and make your heart ache because of it. I tell you their voices soared higher and farther than anybody in a grey place, dares to dream. It is like some beautiful bird flapped into our drab little cage and made these walls dissolve away. For the briefest moment, every last man in Shawshank felt free.'

The music touched their souls in a profound way and seemed momentarily to put them in touch with a transcendent beauty they had never known before.

---

1   The piece is from Mozart's *The Marriage of Figaro*

Eternity in our hearts

The Bible has a whole Old Testament book which probes and investigates this very human longing for transcendent joy. It is the book of *Ecclesiastes*. The writer, who is a very wealthy king, seems to be able to have anything he wants – grand houses, grand designs, gardens, wine, beautiful women, comedy, music, whatever delights the heart of a human being. He tries it all. And he tries it to the full. But he remains unfulfilled and flat. Everything seems somehow empty and meaningless. In fact, the words 'Meaningless, meaningless ... Everything is meaningless' (Ecclesiastes 1:2) become something of a mantra throughout the book. All his experiences and excitements leave him feeling, 'What's the point?' The world is not enough.

But the book gives us a clue as to what Christians would say is going on in our yearnings. In the text, there is a place where the writer declares: 'I have seen the burden God has laid on the human race. He has made everything beautiful in its time. He has also set eternity in the human heart; yet no one can fathom what God has done from beginning to end' (Ecclesiastes 3:10,11).

There is an awareness of eternity and even of God himself somewhere deep in the human psyche. But it is like an empty space, an aching blank, which nothing on earth can fill.

Back to the garden.

What is the explanation of this phenomenon?

The Bible would take us back to the book of Genesis, the creation and Fall of mankind. God created an abundance of living creatures. But mankind was special. Whereas the animals etc. were made according to God's design, mankind's design reflected God himself. We were made as an earthly representation of God's likeness.[2] Not only so, but God himself specifically breathed life into us. It was his spirit that animated us. And more than that, these attributes, unique to the first humans, meant that we were made to relate to God in a way that other creatures could not. We were designed, empowered and enlightened to know God. That is quite a thing! This bestows great dignity upon every human being.

But when mankind rejected God, we excluded ourselves from God's presence. We allied ourselves with what is evil and lost touch with the fount of ultimate beauty, joy, security and satisfaction. We died spiritually.[3] We could say we are hardwired to know the Divine Someone who is no longer there for us. He has withdrawn and hidden himself. And that affects us. Maybe you have a Wi-fi router in your house to service your laptops and iPhones. But imagine a router that can no longer access broadband, and the initiation code has been lost. It is turned on but what the router was made for, it can no longer find. There is no access. Of course, Wi-fi routers don't have emotions, but if they did you can imagine how frustrated they would feel – always searching but never finding. Perhaps that is a small illustration of how we now are as human beings. This, Christianity suggests, is the origin of *sehnsucht*. This is the source of our feeling of lostness and yearning.

And this longing for what we have lost is recognised in the works of the greatest artists ancient and modern. One of the earliest and most famous rock festivals took place near Woodstock, New York State in 1969. It became the inspiration

2 Genesis 1:26,27

3 Genesis 2:17; Genesis 3:6,7,24

and the blueprint for all kinds of events and festivals down the years including Glastonbury.

But there was something of the longing we are talking about behind why so many people gathered which the lyrics of Joni Mitchell's Song *Woodstock*, sum up. There was a yearning in gathering. Why did so many people come? Why was this such a cultural moment? Who were all these human beings who felt that something has gone wrong, and a new kind of society was required? She uses something of the biblical imagery to express it. According to her lyrics people are 'stardust' and 'golden'. But at the same time we are 'caught in the devil's bargain'. And the repeated chorus says that 'we've got to get ourselves back to the garden'.

That sense of having lost the Garden of Eden that we need to find again, is bound into the essence of what it is to be human.

A psychological explanation?

As mentioned at the beginning of this chapter, many secular thinkers would explain this phenomenon of longing as simply a reaction to the pain and seeming precarious nature of our existence. We long for everything to be alright. We long for a 'God' who is greater than this seemingly random world, who can overcome the world, who will guarantee our eventual comfort and survival. In childhood and youth, we are carefree. But at some point in time we realise just how fragile and insecure our lives actually are and we long for that innocent security we once knew and feel as if we have lost. So, secularism would say, God is just a father figure we have invented and projected onto the universe to make us feel safe. We long for a father who will look after us because we know we can't ultimately look after ourselves.

It seems like a viable argument. It appears to be a psychological explanation which might demolish Christianity and all belief in God. And it is on these grounds that many people dismiss Christian faith and refuse to give it a second thought. Christians are just weak people who can't face the bleakness of reality in a pitiless universe and so have dreamed up God. That's the accusation.

Enter Agatha Christie

But is it true? Even apart from the evidence we looked at in chapter 1, if we take a moment to think about this dismissal of God, we find that it doesn't actually stand up, even on its own terms. Why do I say that? Here are three considerations:

First, suppose we do accept that our world is a painful and scary place and that this might well give us a motive for inventing a God. But having a motive doesn't mean that we did it and that it is the true explanation. Think about Agatha Christie, the great writer of murder mysteries. Often as her detective novels unfold and gather pace many suspects present themselves as having perhaps committed the murder. They all have reasons as to why they may have done the victim to death. But having a motive is insufficient to prove culpability. There has to be more concrete evidence. An author of crime fiction who thought that establishing motive was enough to identify the murderer would not sell many books. It is far too simplistic. Similarly, to think that the argument against God can be concluded just because people might have a motive for inventing him is a failure of logic.

Second, such an argument cuts both ways. It could equally well be argued that atheists have a motive behind their belief that there is no God. Maybe they have, even unconsciously, decided that they do not like the idea of a Supreme Being who might hold them accountable for the way they have lived their lives. Perhaps that is why they argue so vehemently that God does not exist. It is not so much to do with the facts as with their psychological needs.

The book *Faith of the Fatherless: The Psychology of Atheism,* published originally in 1999, was written by Paul Vitz, Professor Emeritus of Psychology at New York University.[4] In the work, the author proposes that having a defective or absent father makes it much harder to believe in God. Most of the book examines the biographies of many prominent atheists. These include people like Freidrich Neitzche, Jean-Paul Sartre, H. G. Wells and Richard Dawkins. Vitz produces strong evidence that in nearly every case they had abusive, weak, distant or absent fathers. If their father was a defective character who let them down, the last thing they want to believe in, is a Father in heaven.

Of course, this line of thinking doesn't prove the case for God one way or the other. But what it does do is to show that if you are going to accept a psychological explanation of faith in God, be aware it backfires.

Third, if the need for feeling secure was the motivation would you invent a God like the God of the Bible? The God of the Bible is a God of love, but that is not all he is. He is a God who judges sin and is implacably opposed to all evil. If you were

---

4   *Faith of the Fatherless: The psychology of atheism,* Paul C. Vitz, Second edition, Ignatius Press, 2013

inventing a God simply to act as a psychological Zimmer-frame to lean on in the face of the harsh realities of life, you would invent the God of the Universalist – not the God of the Bible. The Universalist God embodies the idea that no matter what we do, he loves us, and will make sure it is alright for everyone in the end. But the problem is that is certainly not what Jesus taught. He does offer words of comfort: 'Come to me, all you who are weary and burdened, and I will give you rest' (Matthew 11:28). But he also speaks words of warning which resound in our consciences: 'Enter through the narrow gate. For wide is the gate and broad is the road that leads to destruction, and many enter through it. But small is the gate and narrow the road that leads to life, and only a few find it' (Matthew 7:13,14). That really doesn't read like a panacea. It doesn't look like an 'everything will be okay for you in the end' promise.

There is more that could be said. But for reasons like these the idea that God did not make us but that we made him in order to make us feel better proves simplistic and lamentably unsatisfactory.

The Father and the Trinity

Christianity would tell us that God is actually there and the reason for our longing for something beyond ourselves is that we are out of touch with him. Further, Christianity would say that this God is a Father. He reveals himself as a Father, and Christians experience him as a Father.

But before we go any further, we have to say that this is not all God is. There is something about God that it is impossible for us to get our heads around. He is mysterious.[5] He is one God in three Persons. He is the Father, the Son and the Holy Spirit, but one God. The word Trinity is used in theology. The Father, the Son and the Spirit are equal in power and glory. Yet the Father is to be distinguished from the Son and the Son is to be distinguished from the Spirit and the Spirit is to be distinguished from the Father. However, in a way we cannot fathom there are not three Gods but only one. If we are going to get anywhere in thinking about God, Christianity would tell us that we should not let ourselves be put off by this conundrum. It seems irrational but Christians would prefer to say it is supra-rational i.e., that God's mode of existence is real but beyond our human understanding.

However, let me make three short comments which hopefully will help.

First, this truth of the Trinity is in the Bible. For example, at the end of Matthew's Gospel, the risen Jesus tells his disciples to preach the gospel and make Christian disciples across the nations of the world. Those disciples are to identify themselves as they are baptised, 'in the name of the Father and of the Son and of the Holy Spirit' (Matthew 28:19). Notice the three Persons of the Trinity are identified, but their name is singular, not plural.[6] It is 'name' not 'names'.

Second, although there are no foolproof analogies for the Trinity, it does help me as someone with a mathematical background to think of an object known as a Mobius strip. It

---

5 Of course, some readers might object to me using masculine pronouns with regard to God but bear with me. I am not trying to be provocative or to imply that women are lesser persons than men. I am only using the words the Bible uses.

6 See also Romans 1:1–4; 2 Corinthians 13:14; Ephesians 2:18.

is a surface that can be formed by taking a strip of paper and attaching the ends of it together after giving it a half-twist. Contemplating the Trinity we struggle with the idea of three being one and one being three. But in the geometry of the Mobius strip we find that it can be said to have just one side and one edge, while at the same time it also obviously has two sides and two edges. It is both two and one simultaneously. This doesn't in any way solve the mystery of the Trinity, but it might help us to see that it is not totally beyond reason.

Third, if God is truly God then we should expect there to be aspects of his Being that are simply beyond us. Someone has helpfully put it like this: 'If I could understand everything about God, I would be God myself.' The fact that we are left nonplussed by the Being of God is something we ought to have expected if he is real. He is the Creator not a creature. He is God.

What kind of Father?

God is the supreme authority and the ultimate good. We expect him to have titles such as 'Lord' or 'King' but Jesus especially focuses on the radical truth of God as Father. In the Gospels, the biblical 'biographies' of Jesus, when Jesus refers to God as his Father this is often taken as an occasion for offence to be taken by his critics. But he not only speaks of God as his Father, but of his followers as God's children.

According to Jesus, Christians are not just those created by God, but have been brought into the family of God – back into a living relationship with him through Jesus. What kind of Father is God for his children? If, for the moment we take the Gospels as reliable records of Jesus' life and teaching, we get a good idea of the answer by reflecting on the well-known prayer that Jesus taught his disciples to pray.[7] We often call it 'The Lord's Prayer.'

> Our Father in heaven
> hallowed be your name,
> your kingdom come,
> your will be done,
> on earth as it is in heaven.
> Give us today our daily bread.
> And forgive us our debts (sins),
> as we also have forgiven our debtors (those who sin against us).
> And lead us not into temptation, but deliver us from the evil one.
>
> Matthew 6:9–13 (also found in Luke 11:2–4)

Considering this short prayer enables us to briefly draw a thumbnail sketch of the kind of Father God is. He is a God who loves us, as a father does his children. He is worthy of honour and worship and obedience, because, implicitly understood, he is wise and good. He is a father who provides for his family. He is a father who corrects us but who forgives our wrongdoings and expects us to forgive others. He is a father to whom we can look for direction and leading, and is able to rescue us from the evil, which as we have seen previously, besets us all.

When we find God as our Father, or rather are found by him, we can expect to be awed by his greatness, accepted, loved, forgiven, provided for and rescued. Here is the transcendent satisfaction and security we long for. The biblical Psalmist, King David, writes: 'One thing I ask from the LORD, this only do I seek: that I may dwell in the house of the LORD all the days of

---

7 We pick up on the historicity of the Gospels in the next chapter.

my life, to gaze upon the beauty of the LORD and to seek him in his temple' (Psalm 27:4). Here is a man who having found God, is thrilled to the depths of his heart. Elsewhere he sings, 'Great is the LORD and most worthy of praise; his greatness no one can fathom' (Psalm 145:3).

But be careful. Because this God meets all our deepest needs it is tempting, as we have seen that secular people argue, that we must have made him up. But that would be like saying that because the ambulance and its paramedics are perfectly suited to save a casualty, that they must be too good to be true. The fallacy of this way of thinking is obvious. God is real and if he made us in the first place, as the evidence positively suggests, it should not surprise us that he is able to fully address our deepest needs.

Experience of God as our Father is a most wonderful thing. We must not exaggerate the spiritual joy of the Christian life, for as the apostle Paul tells us, in this present life we 'see only a reflection as in a mirror', and not 'face to face' (1 Corinthians 13:12). But on the other hand, we must not have too low an expectation of the ways in which God can draw near. He is able to fill us with 'joy unspeakable and full of glory' (1 Peter 1:8, KJV). Here is a brief quotation from the diary of the eighteenth century English evangelist George Whitefield which does indicate to us how glorious God is:

> Could the trees of a certain wood near Stonehouse speak, they would tell what sweet communion I and some others enjoyed with the ever-blessed God there. Sometimes, as I was walking, my soul would make such sallies as thought it would go out of the body. At other times I would be so overpowered with a sense of God's Infinite Majesty that I would be constrained to throw myself on the ground and

> offer my soul as a blank in His hands, to write on it what
> He pleased ...[8]

To know God as our Father it to know the deepest of joys.
The unknown joy we have longed for, and nothing in this world
can satisfy, is found in God.

Coming to the Father

How can we come to the Father? It is only possible through his
Son, Jesus Christ, as we will explain in the next chapter. But
Jesus does teach very clearly about the attitude of heart and
mind in which we must come.

We come as sinners. We come not as those who are entitled
or see themselves as somehow deserving of a relationship with
God. We do not rely on our supposed merits, piety or good
deeds. To approach God self-righteously is a total mistake. We
come to him in prayer, sorrowfully confessing our collusion
with evil our need for pure, undeserved mercy. Here is a
portion of Luke's Gospel which is underlines what is being said.

> To some who were confident of their own righteousness
> and looked down on everyone else, Jesus told this parable:
> "Two men went up to the temple to pray, one a Pharisee
> and one a tax-collector.
> The Pharisee stood up and prayed about himself: 'God,
> I thank you that I am not like other people – robbers,
> evildoers, adulterers – or even like this tax-collector. I fast
> twice a week and give (away) a tenth of all I get.'
> But the tax-collector stood at a distance. He would not
> even look up to heaven, but beat his breast and said, "God,
> have mercy on me, a sinner."
> I tell you that this man, rather than the other, went home

---

8 George Whitefield, *Journals*, Banner of Truth, 1986, page 83–84

justified (right) before God.
For all those who exalt themselves will be humbled, and
those who humble themselves will be exalted."

Luke 18:9–14

In first century Palestine, where Jesus lived, the tax-collectors were, more often than not, collaborators with the occupying Roman army, and were infamous among the ordinary people for their cheating and greed. And yet Jesus explains here that even such a person can be forgiven and accepted by God when they are convicted of the wrong they have done and humbly ask God for mercy.

The Father's welcome

Coming to God cannot be formulaic. There is no recitation of a form of words which will do. It is a matter of a broken heart which confesses its abject neediness and looks to God to step in, and accept us, in his kindness and love.

Here is another parable, specifically involving a father, that Jesus told which insists on the same point. Jesus had been eating with men and women well-known for their loose morals. In the culture of the day to eat with someone was a sign of fellowship and friendship. How could Jesus, who claimed to be God's Son, possibly befriend and extend a welcome to such people? Those who considered themselves respectable and decent people were outraged.

Jesus continued: "There was a man who had two sons.
The younger one said to his father, 'Father, give me my share of the estate.'
So, he divided his property between them.
Not long after, the younger son got together all he had, set off for a distant country and there squandered his wealth

in wild living.

After he had spent everything, there was a severe famine in that whole country, and he began to be in need. So he went and hired himself out to a citizen of that country, who sent him to his fields to feed pigs. He longed to fill his stomach with the pods that the pigs were eating, but no one gave him anything.

When he came to his senses, he said, 'How many of my father's hired servants have food to spare, and here I am starving to death! I will set out and go back to my father and say to him: Father, I have sinned against heaven and against you. I am no longer worthy to be called your son; make me like one of your hired servants.' So he got up and went to his father.

But while he was still a long way off, his father saw him and was filled with compassion for him; he ran to his son, threw his arms around him and kissed him.

The son said to him, 'Father, I have sinned against heaven and against you. I am no longer worthy to be called your son.'

But the father said to his servants, 'Quick! Bring the best robe and put it on him. Put a ring on his finger and sandals on his feet. Bring the fattened calf and kill it. Let's have a feast and celebrate. For this son of mine was dead and is alive again; he was lost and is found."

Luke 15:11-24

We come to God, like the younger son in the parable, to find mercy. He had sinned terribly. To ask for his inheritance like that was in effect to say 'Father, I wish you were dead, so I can have what is coming to me!' It would break any father's heart to be treated like that by a child he loved. It was embarrassing beyond measure. What would the rest of the community think about a family where such a thing had happened? Further, the young son had wasted half the family's fortune on his selfish lifestyle. What he has done is unspeakably offensive. And yet, Jesus' story tells us, there is forgiveness for him as, broken and humble, he returns to his father. In fact, there is more than forgiveness for him. It is clear that the father is pleased and delighted that his son has returned. There's a celebration.

As you can imagine, Jesus' parable goes on to say that the older brother was livid at the father's welcome for the young villain. This reflects the annoyance of the respectable people at Jesus' befriending sinners. But the parable clearly portrays God as a forgiving father.

He is a Father who forgives those who have collaborated with evil and welcomes even those who have been rebels against him – people like us.

But how can a God who is against all evil do that? That brings us to think about God's Son, Jesus Christ.

Chapter 4:
The Son who rescues us

As a young postgraduate in the 1970s, I visited Israel for a physics conference at the Technion research institute in Haifa. The symposium, under radiant skies and next to the glistening Mediterranean, attracted many researchers and lasted about ten days. There were erudite lectures on the latest research in spectroscopy given by scientists from across the world including Russia and the USA, which during those Cold War years gave a certain edge to things.

But while I was there, I took the opportunity at the weekends, to visit a number of sites which are referred to in the Bible, especially those relating to the ministry of Jesus both in Galilee and Jerusalem.

I remember vividly standing on an ancient stone pavement which archaeologists had uncovered, off one of the side-streets of old Jerusalem. Our guide was rather over-egging things for the tourists as he talked about this pavement being the stone pavement referred to in John's Gospel named 'Gabbatha' in Aramaic, where Pontius Pilate handed Jesus over to his enemies to be crucified.[1] For a start the Jerusalem which Jesus knew was destroyed by the Roman army in AD 70 following the Jewish uprising. The city was rebuilt by the Emperor Hadrian in AD 135 and no doubt some of the older paving slabs reused. But there was no way to be sure that this was the place where Jesus stood when the Roman procurator mockingly announced to the crowds, 'Here is your king'.[2]

However, among the Roman flagstones, in various parts of the pavement, clearly to be seen, are places where legionaries carved lines and squares for the games they played in their off-duty or idle moments. One set of marks, with a crown and the letter 'B' in the centre (standing for *basileus* the Greek word for 'king'), has been identified as the 'King's Game', in which soldiers gambled using dice. While we cannot be sure this is the precise location where Jesus was condemned to death, it does make the report, recorded in three of the four Gospels, of the Roman soldiers gambling for Jesus' robe look entirely realistic.[3]

Our history

Was Jesus a real person? How can we find reliable information about him? In order to progress with our investigation of Christianity, we have to think about such questions.

The four Gospels, short biographies of Jesus which begin the New Testament, are unequivocal about placing him in world history – our history. According to them, Jesus is not a mythical figure or simply an idea. Though he emerged from an

---

1   John 19:13

2   John 19:14

3   Matthew 27:35; Mark 15:23; John 19:24

obscure social background in Galilee, Northern Palestine, the writers place him squarely in the times and amid the politics of historical characters whose existence no rational person would ever doubt. They tell us that:

- He was born during the reign (37 BC – 4 BC) of Herod the Great, while Caesar Augustus was Roman emperor (27 BC – AD 14).[4]
- His three-year ministry took place around AD 30 according to our calendar. This was when Herod Antipas was ruler of Galilee and Perea (4 BC – AD 39).
- His death by crucifixion occurred while Pontius Pilate was the Roman governor of Palestine (AD 26/27 – AD 36/37).

The Gospel writers claim to give eyewitness accounts, their own and those of others, of what Jesus said and did. The apostle John, writer of the fourth Gospel, referring to Jesus as 'the Word' puts it like this:

> The Word became flesh and made his dwelling among us. We have seen his glory, the glory of the one and only Son, who came from the Father, full of grace and truth.
>
> John 1:14

'We have seen' he says. Later he writes to a group of Christians in his first letter and explains his own eyewitness experience of Jesus like this:

> That which was from the beginning, which we have heard, which we have seen with our eyes, which we have looked at and our hands have touched – this we proclaim concerning the Word of life.

---

4   The anachronism in dates here is due to historical calendar changes.

> The life appeared; we have seen it and testify to it, and we
> proclaim to you the eternal life, which was with the Father
> and has appeared to us.
>
> 1 John 1:1–2

The writer of the third Gospel, Luke, was not himself an eyewitness of Jesus. But he was a thorough researcher. This is how he begins his Gospel:

> Many have undertaken to draw up an account of the things
> that have been fulfilled among us, just as they were handed
> down to us by those who from the first were eyewitnesses
> and servants of the word.
> With this in mind, since I myself have carefully investigated
> everything from the beginning, I too decided to write an
> orderly account for you, most excellent Theophilus, so that
> you may know the certainty of the things you have been
> taught.
>
> Luke 1:1–4

Whether Theophilus was a real person, or, because his name means 'lover of God', Luke was using it as a cipher for his Christian readers, is beside the point. The main thrust is that Luke says he is writing his Gospel out of painstaking research to get to the truth concerning Jesus.

Non-Christian references

The life of Jesus had such a powerful impact on the world of the first century, that though he was born in a poor family in an out of the way part of the Roman Empire – a comparative nobody – yet there are some references to him even in the literature of non-Christians of the day.

For example, in his *Annals of Imperial Rome*, the Roman writer Tacitus (AD 56 – AD 120), speaks about the fact that it was rumoured that the great fire of Rome in AD 64 had been a case of arson: 'To suppress this rumour, Nero fabricated scapegoats – and punished with every refinement the notoriously depraved Christians (as they were popularly called). Their originator, Christ, had been executed in Tiberius' reign by the governor of Judea, Pontius Pilate. But in spite of this temporary setback the deadly superstition had broken out afresh, not only in Judea (where the mischief had started) but even in Rome.'[5]

It is clear that Tacitus is no friend of Christianity. He calls Christians 'depraved', and Christianity a 'deadly superstition' and a 'mischief'. But he is quite clear about the existence of Jesus and his execution when Pontius Pilate was governor of Judea.

Furthermore, Jesus is mentioned on at least a couple of occasions in the *Talmud*. This is the collection of the comments of Jewish rabbis, written between AD 70 – AD 200. One of these declares that 'On the eve of the Passover they hanged Yeshu'.[6] The name 'Yeshu' is the Jewish way of saying 'Jesus'. It seems to confirm both the existence of Jesus and the claim in the Gospels that he was executed during the Passover festival. The word 'hanged' had a wider meaning than the way we think of it today and the New Testament itself uses the word on at least two occasions to refer to crucifixion.[7]

So, there are passing references to Jesus, even in the general literature of the early centuries. But, of course, Christians would say that for a fuller understanding of Jesus and what he stood for, we need to listen to those who actually knew him.

---

5   *The Annals of Imperial Rome*, by Tactitus, Penguin Classics, 1989, page 365

6   For a fuller discussion of this reference see *He Walked Among Us*, by Josh McDowell and Bill Wilson, Alpha/Paternoster, 2000, page 64.

7   Luke 23:39; Galatians 3:13

We need to read (and I hope you will for yourself) the Gospels based on eyewitness accounts.

Marks of reliability

The Gospels claim to be reliable documents. What is the evidence for that? Does, for example, John's assertion of seeing Jesus and Luke's claim to have pursued thorough research stand up to scrutiny?

This makes a fascinating and wide-ranging study in itself – far beyond what can be attempted within the confines this book.[8] However, here are three brief indicators that the Gospels can be trusted. In a sense, we find, these books speak for themselves as to their truth.

First, reading them, you will see that they come across as very much uncontrived. In the first century, Jewish law required two or three witnesses to establish the truth of a situation. It was regular courtroom practice. It should not surprise us therefore that there are four Gospels – more than fulfilling the requirement for witnesses to be taken seriously. These are written by Matthew, Mark, Luke and John, and witness to the life of Jesus.

Matthew and John were among Jesus' followers from the start of his public life. As we have seen, Luke explains that he wrote his Gospel based on thorough investigation – interviewing many people who knew Jesus (very likely including Mary, Jesus' mother). Mark's Gospel probably encapsulates the memories and preaching of Peter, the chief disciple of Jesus. Comparing

---

8 To look at this subject in depth see *The Historical Reliability of the Gospels*, by Craig L. Blomberg, Apollos/IVP, 2007

and contrasting the four Gospels, it is clear there has been no attempt to plan or manage or coordinate what is said. The writers do not seem to have colluded in order to 'get the story straight'. Yet they do all tell the same story. Though there is some overlap, especially between the first three Gospels, they come across very much as independent accounts of the life of Jesus. In fact, at a few points, they appear to slightly contradict each other. For example, in a couple of instances, where Mark tells of Jesus dealing with one person, Matthew refers to two.[9] Again, the accounts of the resurrection of Jesus seem almost contradictory unless you do some very intense research, but they can be reconciled.[10] These are the marks of independent reports. They don't always speak the same way, but they are all describing the same occurrence. This, in itself, has the ring of truth about it.

Second, the fact that, as a Jew, Jesus' first language would have been Aramaic, provides us with more evidence of the faithfulness of the Gospels. The whole New Testament, including the Gospels, was written in Koine Greek, the common language of the Roman empire. From early on, Christianity spread across many lands surrounding the Eastern end of the Mediterranean and to many Gentile people who knew little of the Jewish language. So, to use the *lingua franca* of the time made sense as apostles wrote internationally to the different churches and the story of Jesus was shared.

But there is no lack of evidence in, for example, Mark's Gospel that much of the material originally existed in Aramaic

---

9 Compare for example, Matthew 8:28-34 with Mark 5:1-20.

10 See *Easter Enigma: Do the Resurrection stories contradict one another?* by John Wenham, Paternoster, 1984

with the writer's Greek preserving the Aramaic way of saying things and sometimes actual Aramaic words.[11] This, in itself, indicates that Mark (with Peter) was doing his best to carefully convey what actually happened. But we can go further. The late Professor F. F. Bruce writes this: 'Another interesting fact which comes to light when we try to reconstruct the original Aramaic in which our Lord's sayings in all the Gospels were spoken is that many of these exhibit poetical features. Even in a translation we can see how full they are of parallelism, which is so constant a mark of Old Testament poetry. When they are turned into Aramaic, however, they are seen to be marked by regular poetical rhythm, and even, at times, rhyme'.[12] If Jesus wanted his teaching to be remembered, his use of poetry is easily explained. This underlying Aramaic poetry is another weighty piece of evidence that his teaching has been preserved for us as originally given.

Third, the geographical knowledge of the Gospel writers is so abundant and precise as to show that they were writers who knew what they were talking about. There are, of course, other documents purporting to be 'Gospels'. These were famously championed in Dan Brown's fictional mystery *The Da Vinci Code* published in 2003 and later made into a film – books like *The Gospel of Thomas* and *The Gospel of Mary*. These are associated with the religious philosophy known as Gnosticism and were probably written sometime in the second century after Christ.

One of the telling factors that shows these Gnostic Gospels to be suspect, is their writers' comparative lack of geographical knowledge. Whereas Matthew, Mark, Luke and John mention

---

11 For example, Mark 5:41; 7:34; 15:22

12 *The New Testament Documents*, by F. F. Bruce, IVF,1968, page 39

not just the big towns but all kinds of out of the way places in connection with Jesus' ministry, the Gnostic Gospels mention little more than Jerusalem. Exact geographical knowledge is the mark of an eyewitness, whereas the Gnostic Gospels speak very generally. Peter J. Williams, Principal of Tyndale House, Cambridge writes as follows: 'The four Gospels demonstrate familiarity with the geography of the places they write about. In total they mention twenty-six towns: sixteen in Matthew and Luke and thirteen in Mark and John. Among the towns listed are not only famous places – like the religious capital, Jerusalem – but also small villages, such as Bethany (all four Gospels) and Bethphage (Matthew, Mark and Luke). In John we find numerous minor villages mentioned: Aenon, Cana, Ephraim, Salim and Sychar. It is worth reflecting on how such knowledge could be obtained. In principle, one might get it through personal experience, reading, or hearing. However, it does not seem that the Gospel writers could have simply obtained their information from reading. No known sources hold together the particular set of information they have; and, besides, we would have to suppose that they undertook a level of literary research quite unparalleled in ancient history.'[13]

Once again, we have a clear indication that the Gospel writers were there with Jesus as he travelled around preaching or they knew those who were. They were eyewitnesses themselves or they interviewed carefully others who were.

Even from these quick considerations we are encouraged to see that the Gospels have integrity. If we want to know about Jesus, we can turn to them for reliable information.

---

13 *Can We Trust The Gospels?* By Peter J. Williams, Crossway, 2018, page 55

Who was Jesus?

We have thought a little about the Jewish historical background of Jesus and his use of the Aramaic language in his preaching. This raises in our minds a question as to whether it is possible to get behind the Greek text of the New Testament back to something more 'original'.

Starting in the late eighteenth century, some academics began what came to be known as 'the quest for the historical Jesus'. The hope driving these Enlightenment scholars, influenced by the rationalism of the day, was that they might be able to find evidence that it is legitimate to dispense with the miracles of Jesus. A much more acceptable 'Christianity' would emerge if the wonder working side of Jesus ministry could be shown to have been generated from the Christian rumour mill and the stories of Jesus healing people and casting out demons were simply exaggerations added to the 'legend' of Jesus by over enthusiastic believers of a later period. It would be far easier to see Jesus simply as a highly gifted yet ordinary man who taught the Fatherhood of God and that mankind are all brothers and sisters and we should love each other.

However, the quest for the 'historical Jesus' has gone on now for over 200 years and nothing supporting the merely human Jesus has ever been found or shown to fit the evidence. The search has all but petered out. Again, Professor F. F. Bruce sums up the situation: 'No matter how far back we may press our researches into the roots of the gospel story, no matter how we may classify the gospel material, we never arrive at a non-supernatural Jesus'.[14]

---

14 *Ibid*, page 33

The Son of God

The New Testament's claim is that though at one level, Jesus was an ordinary man, a carpenter from Nazareth, at another level he was, simultaneously, the Son of God, in fact God become man. If this is true, then it would be hard not to expect to find something unusual, even supernatural, about his life.

What is striking is that according to the Gospels, the Jewish religious authorities who opposed Jesus never disputed Jesus' miracles. It seems that they were obvious to everyone. Instead of denying the miracles, they tried to turn people against Jesus by saying that his miraculous powers were not from God but from the devil. 'The teachers of the law who came down from Jerusalem said, "He is possessed by Beelzebub! By the prince of demons, he is driving out demons."'[15] Jesus himself dismissed this accusation with a one-liner: 'If a kingdom is divided against itself, that kingdom cannot stand'.[16] If this were true it would be a very bad strategy on Satan's part.

We find the opposition to Jesus and Christianity in the years subsequent to his crucifixion continuing in the Jewish writings of the time. But again, there still seems to be an acceptance of his supernatural powers. The reference in the *Talmud* which spoke of the 'hanging' of Jesus, to which we have already referred, is like this. It speaks of an announcer going around for 40 days prior to the crucifixion saying that 'he is going to be stoned, because he practised sorcery and enticed and led Israel astray'. While this does not accord with what the Gospels say, it

---

15 Mark 3:22
16 Mark 3:23

nevertheless identifies Jesus as one who performed miracles of some sort, designating him as a 'sorcerer'.[17]

There is also a similar, though disputed passage, in *The Antiquities of the Jews* by the first century Jewish historian Josephus in which Jesus is referred to as 'a doer of marvellous deeds'.[18]

The dominance of the cross

Yet though the Gospel writers portray Jesus as being both a great ethical teacher and a worker of miracles who brought restoration and healing to broken people, that is not where the emphasis of any of the Gospels falls. Rather all four of these mini biographies of Jesus focus on the last week of his life culminating in his death on the cross and his resurrection.

In Matthew, which has 28 chapters, the events of the so-called 'Passion Week' begin in chapter 21 and carry through more or less to the end. That is a quarter of the book. Mark and Luke are similar. John's Gospel, comprising of 21 chapters, begins the story of the days leading up to the cross certainly by chapter 12. This is getting on for half of the Gospel.

The crucifixion of Jesus, followed by his resurrection three days later, dominates the narrative. In this way the writers of the four accounts of Jesus' life are signalling quite clearly that if we want to understand the central feature of Jesus' mission then we must concentrate on the cross.

---

17 *Babylonian Talmud*, Sanhedrin 43a

18 *Antiquities of the Jews*, by Josephus, book 18, chapter 3, paragraph 3

The story of the cross

Matthew, Mark, Luke and John explain how Jesus came to Jerusalem for the Jewish feast of Passover. Having caused such a stir by his miracles and by his exposing the hypocrisy of the religious establishment, the Jewish hierarchy of the time determined to have him killed. However, such was the popularity of Jesus with many of the ordinary people that the authorities needed to arrest Jesus secretly lest they provoked a riot. And then they needed to manipulate the situation to ensure that the occupying Roman authorities would agree to his execution. To accomplish this, they managed to subvert one of Jesus' central group of twelve disciples, Judas Iscariot, bribing him into leading them to where Jesus usually spent the night in Jerusalem.

Jesus was successfully arrested at night in the Garden of Gethsemane on the Mount of Olives just outside the city boundary. He was then brought before a kangaroo court of religious leaders, and quickly condemned for blasphemy, for failing to deny that he was the Son of God (Matthew 26:63–66). In the early morning Jesus was taken to the Roman Procurator, Pontius Pilate, and the death penalty demanded. Finding no grounds in Roman law for execution, Pilate prevaricated. But the canny Jerusalem leaders seemed to know that Pilate's political capital was in the balance with his masters in Rome. Though Jesus had made it clear that his kingdom is not of this world much was made of his claim to kingship as if it were some kind of treason against the emperor.[19] The leaders and their lackies shouted, 'If you let this man go, you are no friend

---

19 John 18:36

of Caesar. Anyone who claims to be a king opposes Caesar.'[20] With his career in jeopardy, at this Pilate's resistance collapsed. He literally washed his hands of the affair and Jesus was led away to be crucified.

He was marched to a place just outside the city, popularly known in Aramaic as Golgotha (the place of the skull), laid on a wooden cross and large nails were hammered through his wrists and his ankles and the gibbet with its victim erected for all to see, while two criminals were crucified alongside him. Over the cross was written the indictment against him, in Aramaic, Latin and Greek, 'Jesus of Nazareth, the King of the Jews'.[21] It was there, with but a few of his followers, mostly women, looking on, that he breathed his last.

Later, a wealthy Jewish man, Joseph of Arimathea, and one of the Jewish Council, Nicodemus, both of whom had been deeply influenced by Jesus, requested that Pontius Pilate allow them to remove the body of Jesus from the cross. They buried him in a nearby garden tomb, rather like a cave, and a huge stone was rolled across the entrance.

The purpose of the cross

The purpose of Jesus death on the cross is sacrificial atonement for the sins of everyone who believes in him. This is the good news Jesus brings to a lost world.

We have already considered, in chapter 3, God the Father's offer of forgiveness and desire to forgive sinners who come back to him. How can he do that? The problem with forgiveness

---

20 John 19:12
21 John 19:19

is 'what happens to justice?' We often find it difficult to forgive others for this very reason. If we forgive those who hurt us, we feel that justice has not been done – they have got away with it and we have just been made fools of. But God is no fool. For him to truly forgive, justice must be done as well. This is the purpose of the cross.

One of the great aims of the Old Testament, the first part of the Bible, is to give us the framework in advance to understand Jesus and his work when he came. One of its great themes is what the theologians call 'substitutionary atonement'. Sin deserves death – even eternal death. But if an individual or indeed the whole nation of God's people in the Old Testament, sinned, they could be forgiven as an animal was sacrificed in their place.

The origin of this practice was rooted in the Passover. (Remember it was the annual feast of Passover when Jesus died.) Some 1400 years before the coming of Jesus, the nation suffered as slaves in Egypt. But God had determined that he would rescue them from their suffering. He would send the angel of death through the land of Egypt and all the firstborn sons of the Egyptians would die – just as the Egyptians had killed the sons of the Israelites.[22] But, of course, the Israelites were sinners too. How could it be right for the angel of death to 'pass over' them? God told Israel that on the night the angel would come they should gather as families, sacrifice a lamb and paint the lamb's blood on the doorposts and lintel of their dwellings. The blood of the lamb symbolised that for the family a death had been died, justice had been done for sin and they

---

22 Exodus 1:16

were effectively forgiven, so that the angel of judgment did not touch them and the nation was led to freedom.

Now, of course, the blood of animals cannot really make up for our involvement in evil as human beings. But the Old Testament looked forward to the coming of one who would thoroughly and properly pay for our sin. Writing around 700 years before Jesus, the prophet Isaiah foresaw it like this:

> Surely he took up our pain
> and bore our suffering,
> yet we considered him punished by God,
> stricken by him, and afflicted. But he was pierced for our transgressions,
> he was crushed for our iniquities;
> the punishment that brought us peace was on him,
> and by his wounds we are healed.
> We all, like sheep, have gone astray,
> each of us has turned to our own way;
> and the LORD has laid on him
> the iniquity of us all.
>
> Isaiah 53:4–6

The one whom Isaiah foresaw was Jesus. One of the earliest exclamations concerning Jesus in John's Gospel is 'Look! The Lamb of God, who takes away the sin of the world'.[23] Jesus had been sent by the Father to sacrifice himself so that we might be forgiven. Jesus came willingly and was able to bear our sins because he had no sins of his own. He was able to die for us, as our substitute, because he is the King who legitimately represents all who submit themselves to him. Further, he was able to pay for all our sins forever and the sins of all the millions of people who trust in him, because though he was human, he

---

23 John 1:29

73

was also divine. Though he was a man he was also the Son of God.

Here is the heart of Christianity – free forgiveness through Christ's atonement on our behalf. It is through his Son that God can forgive us all. This is how we can come back to the Father. This is how we can truly come to know God.

It helps me to think about how a credit card works. We go into a shop, choose an item, tap our card on the machine and take our purchase home with us. But at that point we haven't actually paid for the item. That comes at the end of the month (or whenever your date is). All our debts that have been registered on the card are then properly paid by the bank from our account. The animal sacrifices of the Old Testament could not really pay for human sin. They registered that atonement needed to be made, that blood must be shed, but little more. But the first Good Friday, was the day of full payment. All the accumulated sins of God's Old Testament people were completely atoned for, retrospectively, as Jesus died. And it is similar for those of us who live this side of the cross. We come, repentantly, in prayer to God and confess our sins. But they too have all been paid for, atoned for in advance, by Christ's death on the cross.

The apostle Peter, in his first letter, sums up the good news of the cross like this, 'Christ also suffered once for sins, the righteous for the unrighteous, to bring you to God' (1 Peter 3:18).

The victory of the cross

'But lots of people died by crucifixion under the Roman empire', someone might say, 'how do we know that the death of Jesus was any different from thousands of others?'

That is a fair question and the answer to it is Jesus' resurrection.

Before you dismiss this as totally implausible, I have to say that I am quite sure that you do believe in resurrection, life from the dead. That might astonish you. What do I mean? Think about this. Even if you are the most fervent and committed atheist, what do you believe? As an atheist you believe something like this. In the beginning there was no God and life emerged from a cosmic accident involving ... dead matter and it has been evolving ever since. Yes, in your way of thinking, it may have taken many millions or even billions of years to occur, but actually you believe in life out of death.

If you take exception to what I, as a Christian am saying, the argument between us is not really about whether it is possible for life to come from death – we both believe it does. The argument is simply about how it happens. You believe that life takes a lot of time and a great deal of luck. I believe that life is so complicated that it takes God. But we both believe it happens. Thus, in considering the resurrection of Jesus don't be too quick to dismiss it by saying that what is dead always stays dead, because even on atheistic assumptions, that cannot be true. It cannot be true because there is life all around us.

According to the New Testament, God was clearly deeply involved with Jesus. If this God created life in the first instance, it is not at all impossible that he should raise the dead – even to a new kind of life that is eternal. And it is the resurrection that not only marks out Jesus of Nazareth from all others who died on crosses in the first century, but it becomes the evidence of the fact that Jesus' death really did deal with sin and secure forgiveness. It is sin that cuts us off from our Creator, the God of life. It brings death. Therefore, death itself being overturned indicates that sin has been thoroughly defeated. The resurrection is not a random slice of the spectacular. It is the logical outcome of God's plan to rescue sinners and bring them back to himself. It denotes God's victory.

So, the story of Jesus does not end when his body was put in the tomb on the Friday evening. The women who followed Jesus, who were witnesses of his death, noted the tomb where his body was interred by Joseph of Arimathea. The next day was the Jewish Sabbath, strictly policed by the religious leaders. Nothing that even looked like work could be done. Jesus' burial had to be rushed to avoid the Sabbath restrictions. With no thought of a resurrection, the women intended to sit out the Sabbath, but then return to the grave on the Sunday morning in order to give Jesus' body a proper burial according to the customs of the times. But, early on Sunday morning, when they got to the tomb it was empty. They went and told his bewildered disciples, some of whom went and checked and found things were just as the women had said. And then the reports began to pile up that Jesus had risen and had appeared to various people, even allowing himself to be touched to show he was no mere apparition.

Doubting Thomas
In their scepticism about the resurrection, perhaps Thomas is the disciple with whom the majority of intelligent people most

easily identify. He wasn't going to fall for this nonsense about Jesus being alive. John's Gospel recounts Thomas's experience after the resurrection like this:

> Now Thomas (also known as Didymus), one of the Twelve, was not with the disciples when Jesus came.
> So the other disciples told him, "We have seen the Lord!"
> But he said to them, "Unless I see the nail marks in his hands and put my finger where the nails were, and put my hand into his side, I will not believe."
>
> John 20:24-25

The reference here to Thomas wishing to put his hand into Jesus side is because, in order to make sure that Jesus really was dead, one of the Roman soldiers had thrust a spear into Jesus' side 'bringing a sudden flow of blood and water'.[24]

What was the reason for Thomas's scepticism? It is probably twofold. First, there is the understandable doubt about a man who was certainly dead being brought back to life – it was not and never has been an everyday occurrence. But secondly, did you notice that Thomas was a twin? The word 'Didymus' is the Aramaic word for twin. If we use our imagination a little, we can understand why perhaps Thomas had his doubts. For him, another much more reasonable scenario explained the resurrection. Perhaps Thomas himself could recall many an occasion when people had mistaken him for his twin. Perhaps he and his twin had even played pranks on people using the fact that they looked so alike.

Jesus really had died on the cross and in Thomas's mind, surely these stories of Jesus alive again from the dead were really because the disciples had simply encountered someone

---

24 John 19:34

else who looked almost exactly the same as Jesus. They had seen a 'doppleganger' – a double of the living person of Jesus. Therefore, Thomas did not simply want to meet the person the other disciples said they had met. He wanted to see the unmistakeable bodily scars of his death. He wanted to be certain that the person they said was alive was the same person who had died on the cross. Only then would he believe in the resurrection.

John goes on to tell his readers what happened next to Thomas:

> A week later his disciples were in the house again, and Thomas was with them. Though the doors were locked, Jesus came and stood among them and said, "Peace be with you!" Then he said to Thomas, "Put your finger here; see my hands. Reach out your hand and put it into my side. Stop doubting and believe."
> Thomas said to him, "My Lord and my God."
> Then Jesus told him, "Because you have seen me, you have believed; blessed are those who have not seen and yet have believed."
>
> John 20:26–29

John then comments, referring to the resurrection and back to a number of other miracles recorded elsewhere in his Gospel, and then he finishes off the story of Thomas like this:

> Jesus performed many other signs in the presence of his disciples, which are not recorded in this book.
> But these are written that you may believe that Jesus is the Messiah, the Son of God, and that by believing you may have life in his name.
>
> John 20:30,31

And when John speaks of life in these verses, he means eternal life.

Chapter 5:
The Spirit who remakes us

The first nuclear weapon used in war was the atomic bomb dropped on the Japanese city of Hiroshima on the morning of 6th August 1945. It is arguable that the devastating power of this bomb and the one exploded subsequently over the city of Nagasaki brought WWII to a swift conclusion as the Japanese realised what they were facing and so surrendered unconditionally.

The Hiroshima bomb engulfed the city in a blinding flash of heat and light. In less than a second the temperature at ground level rose to something like 7000 degrees Fahrenheit vaporising people, melting statues and roof tiles. 80,000 people died instantly. Those who survived had horrific burns and even those at some distance who appeared unscathed later died of radiation poisoning. It was an atrocious event which hopefully will never be repeated.

Impossible life

Today there is a museum at Hiroshima commemorating what happened and to visit that place is to be overwhelmed with a sense of sadness and desolation.

Because of the radioactive fall-out in the area following the atomic explosion it was thought highly unlikely, even impossible, that anything would grow in the area perhaps for decades. The future of the city looked bleak.

But that proved wrong. The last exhibit as you leave the Hiroshima museum is a photograph of a little shrub. It burst through the melted and cracked tarmac just a few months after the tragedy. Ordinarily such a tiny bit of vegetation would have gone unnoticed and be dismissed as totally insignificant. But given the situation it looked like a miracle. It meant life was still possible. Harvests might one day ripen again. This small plant became a huge symbol of hope for the remaining Japanese people. Despite the overwhelming disaster and the deadly toxicity of the environment after the bomb, life had sprung up once more.

I think of this as an illustration of the life and power of the Holy Spirit. Previously we have considered the power of evil in the world and in us. The Bible describes the effects of evil as leaving us 'dead in your transgressions and sins'.[1] Left to ourselves, we are spiritually dead to God. We have no more sensitivity towards the things of God than that of a corpse. We are shut in on ourselves, governed by our selfish desires, and in subjection to the power of evil. Our innate cynicism is actually not as rational as we would like to believe. It is rather a

---

1   Ephesians 2:1

symptom of spiritual ruination similar to the landscape of post-atomic-bomb Hiroshima. Sin has left us barren and poisoned spiritually.

But, despite the effects of evil, the Holy Spirit is able to bring us new life through the Lord Jesus Christ. He is able to bring us to faith.

The Spirit of God

The Holy Spirit is the unseen spirit who is God himself. He is the third Person of the Trinity. We have already seen that this mysterious deity who is behind all that is, is three Persons in one God existing in a mode of being beyond our ability to understand. He is the Trinitarian God. God the Father planned salvation before the beginning of time. God the Son established salvation through his incarnation and atonement for our sins. But it is God the Holy Spirit who is at work in applying that salvation to us as individuals. And they are one God.

In particular, the Holy Spirit is the bringer of life. Speaking of all the vast biodiversity of our planet the Old Testament Psalmist says of God, 'When you take away their breath, they die and return to the dust. When you send your Spirit, they are created, and you renew the face of the ground' (Psalm 104:29,30). And it is the Holy Spirit who, through Jesus, can give us spiritual life despite the Hiroshima-like toxicity and ruin of our own hearts. Jesus spoke about our need to be born 'again' – born a second time by the Spirit of God (John 3:1–8).

Following the resurrection, the New Testament tells us that Jesus ascended into heaven until his promised return.[2] But he sent the Holy Spirit to continue on earth and apply his saving work to individuals. In this sense, although the name 'Immanuel' which means 'God with us' was originally given to Jesus at his incarnation, it is the Holy Spirit who is now 'God with us'.

Two of the most telling symbols for the Spirit are those of breath and water. God breathed into the body of Adam to make him a living person. We can think of paramedics carrying out resuscitation on a person who has just died, pumping the heart and breathing into their mouths until life returns. Just so, God can breathe spiritual life into us again by his Spirit. We can think of gardens arid and dead after a long hot summer. But then comes a rainstorm, and it is not long before green shoots of life start to appear and eventually blossom and fruit. Life has come again.

The Holy Spirit has such power – power to bring life, to restore life, to maintain life.

Sometimes that power is shown in what we would call miraculous ways. The ten great plagues of Egypt which were used to bring the Israelites out of slavery despite the might and stubbornness of Pharaoh are referred to in the Bible as being carried out by the 'hand of God' or by the 'arm of God'.[3] Jesus spoke about casting out evil spirits from people 'by the finger

---

2 There is not space in this book to dwell on Christ's return, but see for example Matthew 24:36–41; 2 Peter 3:3–13

3 For example, Exodus 6:1; 7.4; Psalm 136:11,12.

of God'.[4] These too are all metaphors for the power of the Holy Spirit.

Two dynamics at work

Thinking about the work of the Holy Spirit it is profitable to picture two great forces or dynamics in play in our world today. These two prevalent factors are God's judgment and God's salvation.

What is God's judgment at work in our world like at the present time? It is not first of all to do with lightning bolts from heaven or even wars and disasters. God's present judgment is much more subtle than that. His judgment now is that as people have rejected him, he allows them to go their own way without intervening. He lets them make their choices and do what they want to do and reap the consequences.

We find this repeatedly in the Bible. After Israel had been rescued from Egypt the people complained that they only had manna to eat and no meat. Eventually God sent them quail. He gave them what they craved. But whether it was because they were unused to such a rich diet of meat or because they fell to eating the birds without cooking them properly it soon made them terribly sick.[5] Later Israel longed to be like other nations and have a king to fight their battles. Rejecting the prophet Samuel's warning they insisted on this. God gave them what they wanted, but before long they found that many of their kings became oppressors of the people.[6] It is a very just

---

4 Luke 11:20

5 Numbers 11:4–35

6 1 Samuel 8:1–22; 1 Kings 12:1–33

judgment. Who could accuse God of being unfair when people are permitted to do whatever they want? But it ends in disaster.

The landslide

According to the New Testament, this same process of judgment is at work today in every society that rejects God and prefers its own 'wisdom'. This is how the apostle Paul describes what happens:

> The wrath of God is being revealed from heaven against all the godlessness and wickedness of people, who suppress the truth by their wickedness, since what may be known about God is plain to them, because God has made it plain to them.
>
> For since the creation of the world God's invisible qualities—his eternal power and divine nature—have been clearly seen, being understood from what has been made, so that people are without excuse.
>
> For although they knew God, they neither glorified him as God nor gave thanks to him, but their thinking became futile and their foolish hearts were darkened.
>
> Although they claimed to be wise, they became fools and exchanged the glory of the immortal God for images made to look like mortal human being and birds and animals and reptiles.
>
> Therefore God gave them over in the sinful desires of their hearts to sexual impurity for the degrading of their bodies with one another.
>
> They exchanged the truth of God for a lie, and worshipped and served created things rather than the Creator—who is forever praised. Amen.
>
> Because of this, God gave them over to shameful lusts. Even their women exchanged natural relations for unnatural ones.
>
> In the same way the men also abandoned natural relations with women and were inflamed with lust for one another.
>
> Men committed shameful acts with other men, and

received in themselves the due penalty for their error.
Furthermore, since they did not think it worthwhile to
retain the knowledge of God,
So God gave them over to a depraved mind, to do what
ought not to be done.

Romans 1:18–28

Paul goes on to describe a self-centred society, full of boasting, animosity, greed and family breakdown very much like our own. The assurances of the atheist liberal intellectuals of a century or so ago that it would be perfectly possible to kill off God and yet remain committed to the old ethical standards and maintain a 'decent' society have proved false. Instead, the way our Western world is going, it would seem that the apostle Paul knew more accurately how things would go.

This moral demise can be pictured as a kind of societal landslide. We can think of a house on a cliff edge. Coastal erosion is happening. The foundations are undermined. The house begins to tip. It may continue stable in its precarious position for a while. But then it slides again, and then later again, and it is clear what the end will be.

Just so the Christian foundations of Western culture have been undermined by the rejection of God. The plausibility of a moral lifestyle has begun to slip away from under people's feet. A 'feel good' attitude to life takes over and trumps more or less everything. Moral values are relativised and begin to slide. There may for a while be a new agreed set of norms. But then why stop there? There is no solid answer. So, the slide continues.

In his great novel *The Brothers Karamazov* the great Russian novelist Dostoyevsky contemplates the consequences of atheism. "'But what will become of men then?' I asked him,

85

"without God and immortal life? All things are permitted then, they can do what they like?'" Though Dostoyevsky presents this as a question, the implication is that indeed when there is no God, then logically 'everything is permitted'.

The tacit atheism of our society leads people into believing that 'it's my life and I will live it as I please and I'm not going to listen to anyone who says otherwise.' It looks like freedom but actually it is captivity to the desires and urges we find within ourselves. We find ourselves at the beck and call of yearnings and cravings which know no end. And as life becomes self-serving, people are set against each other, and the quality of our lives slides away.

And we are all, in one way or another caught up in this landslide. Very often, it is the women, children, the poor and racial minorities who suffer.

This says the apostle Paul, is God's judgment on a godless world. In some ways it is a merciful judgment. It acts as a judgment in slow motion. It takes time to unfold. It is given in the hope that perhaps people will recognise the bitter fruit of their choices and come to the conclusion that this is not the right way. Whether or not that ever happens is another question.

The Holy Spirit's intervention

Yet to ordinary people whose lives are sliding away into various levels of disappointment, sin and brokenness God the Holy Spirit reaches out. Here is the second great dynamic at work in the world. He intervenes through the good news of Jesus Christ.

This landslide into which people are drawn eventually sweeps them away over the edge of a cliff. The cliff edge is not just that of societal breakdown but a lost eternity without God for individuals. It is the same pattern as we have already seen. People do not want God, so God gives them what they want – but this time it is forever. This is final judgment. The Bible says that it is appointed to us once to die and then the judgment. But as God is the source and provider all that is good – of all love, all vitality, all rest and kindness – to choose to be without God is a disastrous decision. To reject him is to choose hell itself.

But the Holy Spirit intervenes. What does that intervention look like? Jesus himself describes it. Speaking to his disciples of the Holy Spirit, he said:

> When he comes, he will prove the world to be in the wrong about sin and righteousness and judgment:
> about sin, because people do not believe in me;
> about righteousness, because I am going to the Father, where you can see me no longer;
> and about judgment, because the prince of this world now stands condemned.
>
> John 16:8–11

The Holy Spirit's work is first of all a convicting work. To be convicted is to be on the wrong end of a formal verdict of a jury in a court of law that you are guilty of an offence. Our conscience is like a courtroom. When he breaks into someone's life the Holy Spirit awakens the conscience of that person. They become acutely aware that they are sinners. They have not lived the life of love that Jesus lived which they know deep down is right, and they come to a realisation that they are answerable to God for the way they have lived.

When this happened to me, I found it excruciating. But it led to joy in Christ as my life was turned around.

Born in a working-class area of West London, I came from a very non-religious family. I was sent to Sunday school once as a child, didn't like it and never went again. But when I attended the local Grammar School I met a number of youngsters my own age who were Christians and came from Christian families. It was with some of these friends that one Saturday night I went along to a youth rally, where a young man spoke from the Bible on the Ten Commandments – God's basic rules for living. He explained about the claim God our Creator has on our lives, that we should not make ourselves idols of any kind and live for things like money, sex and power. He explained that we should not misuse God's name and keep the Lord's Day as a day set aside for worship. We should honour our parents. We should not murder or commit adultery in act or thought. We should not steal, lie or covet things which were not ours. As he preached, I was confronted with the fact that though I knew that these rules made sense and were basically right, I was nowhere near keeping any of them.

I could have blamed this failure on the area in which I grew up. I could have blamed the fact that my parents didn't go to church. I could have shifted the blame elsewhere in any number of ways. But at heart I knew this 'sin' as the preacher called it, was my own responsibility. I was guilty. This guilt felt so painful that although I am sure the speaker went on to talk about Jesus and salvation, I didn't hear any of that.

I was so distressed that I remember that on the walk home I told my friends how wretched I had been made to feel, that preaching like that which made people feel so guilty ought not to be allowed by law and such meetings ought to be banned.[7]

But it was the Holy Spirit at work in me. It was through this painful experience that I saw my need of Jesus Christ and eventually came to trust him and surrender my life to him, becoming a Christian.

My experience is of course, far from unique, although not everyone has the same amount of pain in conviction. Mine is just one tiny example, out of millions who have walked this same path as they have seen their need of Christ and have found him.

What to do with our guilt

Many people feel guilty in some way about their lives in ordinary ways.

It is worth just stepping back at this point. The secular world includes many people who say 'I cannot forgive myself'. They feel bad about themselves and are not at all sure what to do about it. After all a world without God makes the human self the judge of all things. Secularism tells us that we alone can validate ourselves or decide whether something is good or bad. 'No-one else has the right to tell me what to do. I bet they are not so great themselves,' we are encouraged to tell ourselves.

But very often that argument fails to free people from their guilt. That strange entity called conscience is there whether we like it or not. We sensibly try to untangle false guilt – feeling guilty about things we really have no responsibility for – from

---

7   Of course, with the 'conversion therapy' ban being considered by the Westminster Government, this may yet happen.

true guilt. But we find that even when we do that, not all our guilt will fit into the 'false' category.

At this point let me quote the Christian writer Tim Keller:

> 'But what happens then when the self is weighed down in guilt nonetheless? No outside agent has the power to overturn the sanctions that the self inflicts upon itself. Who has the right to tell the self, "Your evaluation of yourself is wrong?" The Bible reveals the core of this problem: "If our hearts condemn us, we know that God is greater than our hearts," 1 John 3:20. Here is the essence of what Christianity gives us. Only God is the final judge of who we are and what we have done. If – and only if – he is, then God can overrule our heart's guilt and self condemnation. If he says we are forgiven then we are, and we can tell our hearts to quiet themselves. The secular framework, however, has nothing to give the wounded conscience to heal it.'[8]

Even as broken sinful human beings our consciences sometimes speak to us. Because we are broken the conscience doesn't always get things right. It can excuse the inexcusable and make us feel we have failed even when we haven't. But when the Holy Spirit comes, he brings the conscience back into proper focus. We can no longer blame others or minimise our faults. We are brought to see our need of Jesus through whom we can find God's own forgiveness through the cross of Christ. And if God says we are forgiven then we really are.

This is something of what happens to a person when the Holy Spirit intervenes in their lives.

---

8 *Forgive: why should I and how can I?* by Timothy Keller, Hodder & Stoughton, 2022, page 139

The Spirit and our humanity

This talk of the Holy Spirit coming into our lives is not to be misunderstood. When we think of a spirit coming into us, we understandably might be put off. We perhaps think of something parallel to demon possession. Instead of being dominated by evil we might think of someone coming to be taken over by a spirit of religious mania and sectarian superstition.

But that is not what the Spirit's intervention is like at all. If anything, he makes us more 'human' in the right sense, than we ever were before.

The Holy Spirit works on, in and through our normal human faculties. He addresses our consciences, he enlightens our minds, he charms our hearts. He does not 'zap' us or force us in some oppressive way. He made us human beings in the first place and does not violate his own design. He works miraculously but he treats us with integrity as human beings. This is why, for example, the New Testament encourages us to ask all our questions and to use our minds in considering the Christian faith.

The gospel is addressed to our rational minds and to be converted is 'to come to a knowledge of the truth.'[9] Our affections are brought to love the Lord.[10] Our wills have a new concern to follow Jesus and obey his teaching.[11] We find ourselves choosing a godly way of life.

We never manage all this perfectly as Christians, but we have a new direction in life. The landslide of society is going one way, but we now find that we are going the other. We have

---

9 1 Timothy 2:4; John 8:32

10 John 14:15,21,23

11 Mark 8:34

been turned around. Whereas a secular society rejects God, we don't any more. Whereas our contemporaries ignore Jesus, we believe in him. Whereas the culture encourages everyone to live for self and pleasure, we find we have different priorities. We have been turned around, indicating that we have been rescued from the landslide of God's judgment, at present manifesting itself in slow motion.

We see the world in a whole new way too. One young woman who came to Christ in our church told of how different she felt after she had become a Christian. She was on holiday in Cornwall and enjoying surf boarding. She spoke of standing in the surf and sunshine and looking back onto the beach and the green topped cliffs and feeling overwhelmed by the sense that the God who created this wonderful earth was now her Father since her sins had been forgiven through the Lord Jesus Christ. She felt more alive and at home with herself than she had ever done. The Holy Spirit does not suppress or destroy our humanity, rather he enhances it.

Coming to faith

Because of this confluence between our human faculties and what the Holy Spirit does in a person's life we don't have to sit and wait for something to happen to us in order to become Christians.

On frequent occasions in the New Testament people are exhorted to put their faith in the Lord Jesus Christ. They are to trust him and his promises of forgiveness and eternal life as they would a reliable friend.

> Then they asked him, "What must we do to do the works God requires?"

Jesus answered, "The work of God is this: to believe in the one he has sent."

John 6:28,29

Jesus did many other miraculous signs in the presence of his disciples, which are not recorded in this book.
But these are written that you may believe that Jesus is the Christ, the Son of God, and that by believing you may have life in his name.

John 20:30,31

He then brought them out and asked, "Sirs, what must I do to be saved?"
They replied, "Believe in the Lord Jesus, and you will be saved—you and your household."

Acts 16:30,31

We are to choose to put our faith in the Lord Jesus Christ and when we do so, it is a sure sign that the Holy Spirit is at work in us.

True faith is not just an intellectual faith. An intellectual faith which grasps the facts about Jesus and his teaching and believes they are true is good. It is the right place to start. But if it stops short of becoming an active faith which is personal and affects our lives it falls short of our truly trusting Jesus.

True faith is not just a crisis faith. At the beginning of this book, we cited the story of a man in a hurry desperately looking for a parking space and crying out to God. There are others in real life who have called out to God in much more serious circumstances. There is nothing wrong with that. But if once the crisis has past, we forget God, again this fails to be the trust in Christ the New Testament requires of us. The real thing is a personal and permanent faith for every day, not just for the crises.

True faith is not just a Sunday faith. It is good to go to church and to praise God and make friendships with other Christians at the beginning of each week. But if for the rest of our week our faith is basically forgotten or hidden from others, this again is not faith which has been wrought by the Holy Spirit in our lives.

When a person becomes a Christian, they find that they are given a new appetite for the Bible – reading it and hearing it explained. This is because true faith is based on the word of God. This new life in us, which manifests itself as faith in Christ, wants to be fed and it is fed and finds itself stimulated by the Scriptures.

Furthermore, this new faith is active. It does its best to try to put into practice what it understands from God's word. If God's word forbids certain actions as sinful, then someone with real faith will try their best, asking for God's help to turn away from it. If God's word commends a certain action, like caring for others or forgiving others, then true faith will express itself in a person doing their best, praying for help to do that thing.

The fruit of the Spirit

It is in this way that what the Bible calls the 'fruit of the Spirit' begins to grow in our lives. This is the outward evidence that we have real faith and that our lives have been changed by the Holy Spirit.

This is how the apostle Paul contrasts, in fairly stark terms, the difference between life before becoming a Christian with the life we aspire to and try to follow once we become Christians:

> The acts of the sinful nature are obvious: sexual immorality, impurity and debauchery; idolatry and witchcraft; hatred, discord, jealousy, fits of rage, selfish ambition, dissensions, factions, and envy; drunkenness, orgies and the like.
>
> I warn you, as I did before, that those who live like this will not inherit the kingdom of God.
>
> But the fruit of the Spirit is love, joy, peace, forbearance, kindness, goodness, faithfulness, gentleness and self-control.
>
> Against such things there is no law.
>
> Those who belong to Christ Jesus have crucified the flesh with its passions and desires.
>
> Since we live by the Spirit, let us keep in step with the Spirit.
>
> Galatians 5:19–25

This change is an ongoing process for the Christian in this life. The passage from Galatians just quoted is set in the context of an ongoing battle in our hearts and lives between the sinful nature and the Spirit. The sinful nature is still there in us, but so too is the Spirit of God.

Also, notice that the reason we seek to live in ways which reject sin and follow the Spirit is not in order to try to earn acceptance with God. Once we trust in Jesus we are already saved. We seek to live according to the Spirit because of who we now are. Having trusted Christ, we do not belong to the world and its ways. We 'have crucified the sinful nature'. We now belong to Jesus and to God. To live in line with the fruit of the Spirit is to be and to show who we now are – our true identity.

Transformation

There are many people in the world who wish they could be different from how they are at present. It may be that they try to be very respectable people but know that often they let themselves down. They feel like impostors. One the other hand, it may be that they are far from respectable people who have actively pursued the 'acts of the sinful nature' through lust or greed but have found that such a life does not bring happiness or lasting peace. They wish they could change in some way.

The New Testament understands those yearnings for transformation and tells us that although we may have said to ourselves 'I wish I could be different, but I can't' that there is a kind and gracious power, the power of the Holy Spirit who can change anyone as they put their trust in the Lord Jesus Christ.

Ongoing transformation through the work of the Spirit is not mere moralism. It has a different motivation. One of the great works of the Holy Spirit is to make Christ real to us, so that in a spiritual sense our faith becomes sight. Christians find that when they 'see' Jesus in this way they want to be like him. The apostle Paul describes this process as follows:

> Now the Lord is the Spirit, and where the Spirit of the Lord is, there is freedom.
> And we all, who with unveiled faces contemplate the Lord's glory, are being transformed into his image with ever-increasing glory, which comes from the Lord, who is the Spirit.
>
> 2 Corinthians 3:17,18

With this in mind, let me close this chapter by quoting a passage from the diary of David Brainerd, who later became a missionary to the native Americans. Though it was a conversion experience, and one of unusual intensity yet it does connect with what all Christians know at various times to some degree. In July 1739, as he was walking in a solitary place seeking God this is what happened:

Having been thus endeavouring to pray – though, as I thought, very stupid and senseless – for near half an hour; then as I was walking in a dark grove, unspeakable glory seemed to open to the view and apprehension of my soul. I do not mean any external brightness, for I saw no such thing; nor do I intend any imagination of a body of light, somewhere in the third heavens, or anything of that nature; but it was a new inward apprehension or view that I had of God, such as I never had before … I stood still, wondered and admired! I knew I never had seen before any thing comparable to it for excellency and beauty; it was widely different from all the conceptions that ever I had of God, or things divine. I had no particular apprehension of any one Person in the Trinity, either the Father, the Son, or the Holy Ghost; but it appeared to be Divine Glory. My soul rejoiced with joy unspeakable, to see such a God, such a glorious Divine Being; and I was inwardly pleased and satisfied that He should be God over all for ever. My soul was so captivated and delighted with the excellency, loveliness, greatness, and other perfections of God, that I was even swallowed up in Him; a least to the degree, that I had no thought (as I remember) at first, about my own salvation, and scarce reflected that there was such a creature as myself.[12]

A feeling of peace and joy filled his heart and he became thoroughly disposed to serve and honour 'the King of the universe'.[13]

---

12 'David Brainerd', by John Thornbury, in *Five Pioneer Missionaries*, Banner of Truth, 1965, page 24–25

13 ibid

Chapter 6:
Love's argument

In the film *Living* the actor Bill Nighy plays Mr. Williams, a veteran civil servant in 1950s London.[1] As a very correct, bowler-hatted gentleman who commutes to the capital each day on the train, he heads up an administrative department in the London County Council.

The story begins to unfold as he receives a medical diagnosis which tells him that he only has six months to live. On the face of it, this scenario might well make for a very grim piece of cinema. In fact, it turns into the very opposite.

The question is, how will Mr. Williams react to this prognosis? The narrative moves us through a number of phases. There is a scene in which it becomes clear that he is carrying an inordinate number of bottles of sleeping pills in his briefcase. Initially, therefore, it is intimated, he contemplates suicide through an overdose. But then he moves on to the idea of having a last blast of 'fun' – wine, women and song – abandoning himself to the hedonism which, as a gentleman, he

---

1   Screened for the first time in 2022

had always denied himself. But having tried this for a while he is left dissatisfied and distressed.

At last, after meeting up on a few occasions with a female ex-colleague, he comes to see his way forward – and that way is about doing what good he can for other people. It is about love.

A group of mothers, still living among the slums and bomb sites of post-war Britain, have been pestering the LCC for a playground for their children. Mr. Williams' bureaucratic response over the years had consistently been to push them between official departments, fob them off and generally to ignore their request.

But now, Mr. Williams realises that he can only find peace in dying as he does his best to bring joy to others. Other people matter. It dawns on him that a playground would be a place where children would find pleasure and laughter. So, reversing his previous attitude he begins to use all his influence and energy to overcome the huge bureaucratic and practical barriers to give the slum mothers what they have been asking for. He chivvies administrators for the paperwork. He personally takes on high officials. He visits the site, despite the torrential rain, with planners and surveyors. And he gets it done. The playground is built.

One of the final scenes in the film is of Mr. Williams, just before his death, sitting on a swing at night in the empty, newly built playground, with a smile on his face, happier than he had ever been, looking up at the stars. He is imagining the joy the children will know there, and his bringing of that joy somehow seems to fit with the sparkling universe above him. Love and doing good is what life is meant to be about.

The Question

That is a sentiment with which a lot of us will readily and rightly identify. We feel at home with such a notion. However, it leaves us with a question. The question is 'why does love make sense of life?' Or to phrase it another way, 'Why does it make sense that love should be the purpose of human existence?'

We find the answer to that question written large and repeatedly across the New Testament. We could have cited many readings, but we will look at just one such passage. This is part of the first letter of the apostle John to the churches.

> Dear friends, let us love one another, for love comes from God.
> Everyone who loves has been born of God and knows God. Whoever does not love does not know God, because God is love.
> This is how God showed his love among us: He sent his one and only Son into the world that we might live through him.
> This is love: not that we loved God, but that he loved us and sent his Son as an atoning sacrifice for our sins.
> Dear friends, since God so loved us, we ought to love one another.
> No-one has ever seen God, but if we love one another, God lives in us and his love is made complete in us.
>
> 1 John 4:7–12

In these verses the apostle John is telling us that the character of Mr. Williams in *Living* has got it right. Love is what living is meant to be about. What John tells us about love, presents a very strong and practical case for Christianity. We will unpack what John writes using three simple questions. What? Why? Where?

What is love?

We need to be clear about this. Love comes in many different forms. On Valentine's Day we think of romantic love, but there is also compassion for those in need and comradeship between friends and many more aspects of love.

What is the nature of love? What is at the heart of all those things at their best? John takes us to the essence, as he tells us about God's love. 'This is how God showed his love among us: He sent his one and only Son into the world that we might live through him. This is love: not that we loved God, but that he loved us and sent his Son as an atoning sacrifice for our sins.' There are two things here.

First, real love is something freely given. It is not something coerced or manipulated or we earn or pay for. It is not 'you scratch my back and I'll scratch yours'. That isn't love – even in marriage. That is a business contract. No. Real love is freely given. John tells us that we didn't love God, we had done nothing to deserve God's love. In fact, humanity had done everything to deserve God's anger. We have no merit. Despite outward appearances, inwardly we are scheming and selfish sinners. Yet nevertheless he loved us. Freely. Love has a generous spontaneity about it.

Second, real love involves, self-sacrifice for the good of the one we love. At Christmas we remember that God sent his 'one and only Son' (Jesus) into the world that we might live. It is hard to give away something precious. It is harder still when it is unique. It is harder still when it is your only Son. This is deeply costly. Yet God gave his greatest gift for us. Actually, it is even greater than that in this instance. Because the Bible reveals that God is Trinitarian, the Father and the Son are one, it means there is a sense in which God did not simply give another but he gave himself in his love. This is God's extraordinary love for us. He came to sacrifice himself on the cross, to make atonement, for all we have ever done wrong in our lives. He did this so that he might be reconciled to us and we to him.

As we have seen, we are all tainted by evil. We all have a guilty history before this holy God. It separates us from him. That is why he seems so far away. Our personal history is recorded by God's all-seeing search engine. Perhaps we could think of it being parallel to the history on our computers recording what we have logged on to online. But here is God's love, that history has been cleared for everyone who accepts Christ as their Saviour. It is cleared not just in retrospect, but past, present and future. It is cleared not by the touch of a keyboard button. It took a lot more than that. It took Jesus deliberately loading upon himself all our guilt before God his Father, and paying for it, making atonement for it (v10) on the cross when he died.

That is what love is. It is that affectionate free giving of ourselves at real cost for the good of another.

Indeed, all true love has that element of generous and tender self-sacrifice. It is in the great romance scenes. When the man says 'I love you,' this is what he is communicating. When, in Jane Austen's ever-popular novel *Pride and Prejudice*, Mr. D'Arcy says to Elizabeth, 'Please allow me to express how fervently and ardently I admire you,' he doesn't just mean 'I fancy you.' He means, 'I care for you so much, that I will do whatever it takes, make any sacrifice for your happiness. I love you!' That's true romance. And John is telling us if we have forgotten, this is the heart of love. God gave his only Son for us. Earlier in the same letter John has spelled out the same thing in a slightly different way: 'This is how we know what love is: Jesus Christ laid down his life for us.'[2]

Why does love make sense?

If love is that affectionate sacrificing, giving and diminishing of ourselves for another's good, how does that make sense in our world?

In their most sane moments, people know that love makes sense. Nevertheless, secular people get into a real mess when they try to explain *why* such love is so right. And you will not be able to give any reason why we should love, says our section of John's first letter, unless you realise that love has its origins in God. He writes: 'Dear friends, let us love one another for love comes from God. Everyone who loves has been born of God and knows God. Whoever does not love does not know God because God is love.'

You see, if you do not believe in God, but believe that 'Life, the Universe and Everything' came about by pure accident, then self-giving love makes no sense. In a purely material world only 'survival of the fittest' or 'look after number 1' is sensible – not self-sacrifice for the good of someone else. In secular terms, evolutionary success is about gaining advantage over other competitors, not about handing them the advantage.

Some people, realizing that love has no firm foundation in a godless universe, react by saying, 'So what? Does it matter that love doesn't make sense? Isn't the fact that people need

---

2 1 John 3:16

loving enough to make us love?'[3] But this pragmatic argument is actually muddled thinking because it assumes the answer in the question. It doesn't tell us why other people's needs should mean anything to us in the first place. In other words, it has subtly slipped in a bit of Christianity without acknowledging it.

No, says John, love makes sense, because God is love. Why love? The answer is because the ultimate reality is not just energy, time and chance. It is not blind evolution. The ultimate reality is a Person – God who is love as shown as Jesus sacrificed himself for us. When we love, when we show friendship with no strings attached, when we show compassion to the refugee, when we care deeply for another person, we are walking in God's footsteps. We are in touch with ultimate truth – and we feel it in our hearts. That's why love feels so right. That's where our general instinct about love comes from. That's why at the end of the film *Living* we feel that as Mr. Williams has expressed love for others, we have come to a satisfactory conclusion.

And, though I do not wish to be disrespectful to other people of faith, for me this consideration of the origins of love actually makes an argument for Christianity rather than other religions.

Think about religions like Islam or Judaism which see God as unitary – that he is one and nothing else. How can such a God have love in his essence? Before the creation of the world, he would have been solitary, alone and loveless. There was no

---

3   In his book *The Selfish Gene*, arch atheist Richard Dawkins writes, 'We are survival machines – robot vehicles blindly programmed to preserve the selfish molecules known as genes.' But then, realising that people know that love is right but that it has no basis in mere science, he has to resort to simply encouraging people to defy their genetics and love anyway.

'other' to love. But Christianity insists on the mystery of the Trinity. Before time began to be, God was one and yet three Persons, Father, Son and Holy Spirit. Love flows between the Persons of the Trinity from everlasting to everlasting. That means that when the apostle tells us that 'God is love' that love is part of God's essential being, the concept holds together.

Think about Eastern religions such as Hinduism or Buddhism. Central to these belief systems is the law of karma. Karma denotes an unbreakable cycle of cause and effect. It means that for every individual, right actions produce good results and wrong actions produce bad ones. Alongside the idea of reincarnation, that belief tends to put the brakes on loving others. If someone is suffering it is because of wrong actions in a previous life according to karma. Therefore, to try to help them may well be to interfere with the outworking of karma. So, kindness and love for the needy, instead of being in tune with the ultimate truth of the universe, is actually to wrongly intrude against supreme reality.

Where has our thinking led us? It seems that if we believe in love, as we consider its nature and necessity we are being driven towards Jesus. Only Jesus Christ makes sense of love. Why love? The answer is, as John has said, because 'God is love'. So, it's a logical step for John to go on to write, 'Dear friends, since God so loved us, we also ought to love one another'.

Where can we find this God of love?

How can we meet God? If we are intrigued by him, where is he located so that we can begin to find access to him?

John helps us with this question as he closes this paragraph of his letter. We live in sceptical, even cynical days. 'I can't see your God' people declare. 'Where is your God?' comes the question. John's response is 'No-one has ever seen God, but ...' He agrees that God is invisible to us, but he doesn't leave things there.

In fact, John has two answers to that question about where we can find God. He has two verses in his writings which begin the same way, 'No-one has ever seen God, but ...' The one which occurs in his letter is actually his second answer. His first answer is in his Gospel account of the life of Jesus.

In his Gospel he writes, 'No one has ever seen God, but the one and only Son, who is himself God and is in closest relationship with the Father, has made him known' (John 1:18). He is talking about Jesus. Concerning himself, Jesus was able to say, 'Anyone who has seen me has seen the Father.'[4] So, John's first answer concerning where to find God is to tell us to look at Jesus. In him we will see God. We are not living in first century Palestine where we could have gone and literally seen and heard Jesus. But we do have the Gospel accounts of his life, teaching, death and resurrection. If we want to find God, the first place to start is to read those accounts. Begin by opening the New Testament and discover and study what is written there.

But in his first letter, at the close of our paragraph, John gives us a second answer to our question. 'No-one has ever seen God; but if we love one another, God lives in us and his love is made complete in us.' John is writing to Christian churches. When he speaks of 'we' and 'us' it is churches and Christians that he first has in mind. He has told us that God

---

4   John 14:9

is the origin of love, but now he is saying that as that love is worked out – as Christians love each other – God himself will be there. What that means practically is that you will find God in a loving church.

Sadly, there are today many churches which are not loving. You won't find God there. Look for a church which first of all makes the teaching of the Bible, particularly the New Testament which shows us Jesus, central to all it does. But also, it must also be a loving church, which not only looks at Jesus in God's word and hears his teaching but puts it as much as possible into practice. In such a place, among such people you will find God – the God of love. God lives in heaven. But he also lives among the people of a loving church.

Einstein's portrait

There is a painting I saw not long ago in an art shop on an expensive High Street. I could not afford to buy it, but I fell for it. It is a colourful collage, in the middle of which stands the great scientist Albert Einstein with his flowing white locks, grandfatherly moustache and twinkling eyes. But he is not in the laboratory or engaged in physics calculations. He is carrying a placard. Einstein is the man we associate with the equation $E=mc^2$ and with seeking to find the answer to 'life, the universe and everything'. But the artist portrays him protesting that 'Love is the answer.'[5]

---

5   Mr. Brainwash (pseudonym for Thierry Guetta), *Einstein – Love is the Answer*

What gives real meaning, purpose and satisfaction in life is not dead matter and its interactions but living persons and loving relationships. I think we all know this really.

Epilogue:
Steps of faith?

If you have seen something of the cogency of Christianity reader, you may want to take things further. I don't assume that, but nevertheless, I hope that may be the case.

How can you do that? I have no wish to rush anyone into faith before they are ready. But if you feel able, bear with a little advice.

First, prepare yourself for a bumpy ride. There will be difficulties. Once upon a time Christianity was fashionable in the Western world. That is no longer true. For many reasons, some to do with the world's self-regarding viewpoint and some to do with the sins and mistakes of the church, you will find that to express interest in Christian faith today, is likely to make some of your friends and family unsettled and even derisive. Jesus warned the crowds fascinated by his miracles that to become his disciples was likely to involve various degrees of rejection and peer pressure to walk away from him. Though he epitomised love, yet he was crucified. He said, 'If anyone is ashamed of me and my words in this adulterous and sinful generation, the Son of Man will be ashamed of them when he comes in his Father's glory with the holy angels' (Mark 8:38). So, to press on through to a thorough faith in Christ and following him is unlikely to be without a cost of some kind.

Second, prepare yourself for change. Faith in Christ, as we have already intimated, goes hand-in-hand with the Holy Spirit coming into our lives. We can't expect God to really come into our lives and hearts and for everything to remain the same. There will be actions and attitudes which we have grown used to which God will expect us to leave behind. But simultaneously he will begin to introduce us to what Jesus called life 'to the full' (John 10:10). God's love reshapes us as people, not least in giving us new kinds of friends and new kinds of pleasures. On offer is eternal life and a peace and a joy and a contentedness which the world cannot give. But if we are not ready to change and to be changed, such things will pass us by.

Third, begin to try to pray. For a secular person, this may well feel very awkward and even unreal. But tell God where you are. You can even start with a prayer which is quite sceptical – something like 'O God, if you are there, please help me to find you.' Don't simply pray once. Praying such a prayer regularly over a period of time is a sign of sincerity and that you are serious. Sometimes spiritual reality opens up to us slowly. This was how it was with C. S. Lewis who we mentioned at the beginning of this book. As he was still finding his way, he wrote to an old university friend about how his outlook was beginning to change: 'It is not precisely Christianity, though it may turn out that way in the end. I can't express the change better than by saying that whereas once I would have said "Shall I adopt Christianity?", I now wait to see whether it will adopt me, i.e., I know there is another Party in the affair – that I'm playing poker, not Patience, as I once supposed.'[1] Gradually, God was making himself real to him.

Fourth, seek out a church and start to get to know people there. As I have already explained this needs to be a church committed to Christ through the teachings of the New Testament and composed of loving people. It should have the feel of a family of true sisters and brothers. No doubt you will have many questions. But in such a church you will find friends who will take interest in you and with whom you can talk things through. They will be open to teaching you and praying with you as you feel appropriate.

Fifth, if things go so far as you becoming convinced of the truth of the Christian message then you should pray and commit yourself before God to following Christ – learning his teaching and with God's help trying to put it into practice. In the New Testament you will find that when people took that step of faith, they were baptised and became members of a local church.[2] Becoming a Christian is a matter, first of all, of the heart. But throughout the New Testament and church history, baptism has always been the public declaration of one's faith.[3]

****

A healthy scepticism is necessary in a world where you can't always trust people or their promises. But the bottomless pit of

---

1 Quoted in *C. S. Lewis: a biography*, by Roger Lancelyn Green and Walter Hooper, William Collins, 1974, page 106

2 Acts 2:41, Acts 8:14–16; Acts 10:48; Acts 16:33,34

3 Matthew 28:19; Romans 6:3

cynicism is both irrational (we all operate everyday as if certain things are true) and leads only to despair. There is a place for real hope in life. There is truth to be found and it is worth pursuing – especially the truth about Jesus Christ.